Corruptocracy

Isaac Benson Powell

Copyright © 2020 *Isaac Benson Powell*

All rights reserved.

No part of this book may be reproduced in any form without the written permission of the publisher.

ISBN 978-0-9861653-0-6

Dedicated to "tank man".

Changes from previous version of this book.

The title of this book is "**Corruptocracy**", but the original book (published in 2015) was called "**Corruptocracy and Other Bullshit**". The name change is mainly due to Google not allowing the book title in it's advertisements, which greatly affects the ability to sell it.

Five years passed between the original book and this one, and there are a couple of changes between the two, but no chapters were added or removed.

There were many new chapters I thought of writing, but figured if I did that, people would expect new books with new info every few years… and that is not what I intend to do.

The original book was well written, and made it's point. This version is more "advertising friendly", and has a few adjustments here and there.

Table of Contents

[1] Corruptocracy..6
[2] Microsoft's Hiring Practices...12
[3] Racism and Sexism from Apple's CEO..16
[4] Asking for Race, Gender and Age on Employment Application..........18
[5] The Mormon Church Claims that its Priesthood Holders can Heal People...........29
[6] *Yahoo!* Censoring User Comments..33
[7] Santa Clause and the Tooth Fairy...34
[8] Not Using the Metric System in the U.S.A..35
[9] Internet Driven by Advertising..37
[10] Appending Changes to the U.S. Constitution, Instead of Modifying it...............38
[11] Employment Contract that said I Couldn't Say Anything Bad About Company. .41
[12] Unable to Remove Crapware from Computing Devices......................45
[13] Junk Mail..49
[14] Safeway Club Card..52
[15] The "Reboot" of Star Trek...54
[16] Religion vs. Atheism...57
[17] "Single Use" Batteries...61
[18] The Internet Being Hailed as One of the Greatest Inventions of All Time...........63
[19] Closed Source Software Used by the Public....................................66
[20] Microsoft Forcing Everyone to Have an "NSA account" on *Windows* OS.........70
[21] Health Care...73
[22] The Big Lie Students are Taught About Electricity...........................78
[23] College...81
[24] Multiple Human Languages...84
[25] Human Behavior..86
[26] Human Population..88
[27] Microsoft's Contracting Companies...91
[28] Mormon Church's View of Masturbation..96
[29] Anti-Depressant Medications..104
[30] Conclusion...117
Appendix A: The "13 Articles of Faith" of the Mormon Church...............119
Appendix B: Apple CEO's Racist and Sexist Statement..........................121
About the Author..125

[1] Corruptocracy

Once upon a time, on the North American continent of planet Earth, there was a country called *The United States of America*. This country was created after its people got tired of having a king on the other side of the ocean telling them what to do and how much money to give him. This person became king not by doing anything particularly special, but rather just because he fell out of his mother's birth canal and lived long enough to assume the crown.

George, Thomas, Benjamin and a few other people decided they couldn't take the king's bullshit anymore and decided to break away from him. However, replacing one king with another didn't seem like such a bright idea. So they thought long and hard about how to create a government which would actually represent the interests of the people, and not just the interests of a king or other wealthy individuals.

They decided to try out the idea of "democracy", where the citizens (not women or slaves) would get to vote for the individuals who would govern over them, and they would have elections often enough so nobody would govern for too long (like a king).

...and the people lived happily ever after. The End.

Unfortunately, what these well intended people created was a corrupt version of democracy, I like to call "corruptocracy".

These Founding Fathers, as they are often referred to, wrote up a Constitution, which would serve as the blue print for how the country would be governed, how elections were to take place, etc... WHAT these Founding Fathers intended to do, is MUCH more important than HOW they chose to implement this democracy.

The Constitution is not that different than the design of an automobile, and the portion of the U.S. Constitution where it describes how individuals can be elected to office is as poorly designed as a car that catches on fire when it's involved in a minor fender bender. A re-design of this part of the Constitution is needed so bad, that NOTHING else is more important. Without a change, you really are not any better off than people living with kings/queens to rule over them, as you don't really have a democracy of the people. What you currently have is a system that ONLY represents the wealthy. Sure, when they fuck up really bad with some new law, tax, or invasion of privacy and piss off the general population bad enough, these corrupt politicians know to back track a little, but so do most kings and queens, at least the ones that like their heads attached to their bodies.

So, what is wrong with the way we currently elect our overlords? **Money in the election process!** The political leaders of *The United States of America* are corrupt to their very core, and I can prove it with a simple analogy.

Let's say you are driving down the road one day and get pulled over by a police officer for speeding. For one reason or another you really don't want a ticket and offer the police officer $50 to let you go without one. Offering money to a police officer to change their behavior is considered a bribe (and is illegal). If the police officer accepts the money, I would consider him/her to be corrupt.

The same thing occurs in the political election process of *The United States of America*. However, instead of being called "bribes", they're called "campaign contributions". They really are the exact same thing though. People give money to politicians as campaign contributions and in return they expect the politician to support their cause. This creates a system where money drives the decision making process of politicians, and that is corruption. Instead of $50, politicians deal with millions of dollars to get elected.

Solution: Money-Free Election

The election process I'm about to describe is very different from what you're used to, but as I explain how it works, ask yourself these questions:

1. Are the politicians members of the community they represent?
2. Does money give one candidate an advantage over another?
3. Does the public get to vote for the people who will govern over them?
4. Is this a democratic election process?

For any given public office (President, Congress, Governor, etc...), the government would randomly select 100 citizens over the age of 35, from the population the office represents, as candidates for that particular office.

A few elimination rounds would be held where we slowly reduce the number of candidates, from 100 → 50 → 10 → 1. After each elimination round, the pool of candidates will theoretically get better and better, until you're left with one person who is well qualified to fill the position.

As far as each candidate being able to get their message out to the public, we would have one central website where each candidate would have a chance to state their opinions on various topics and to make their case why they should be elected. To ensure freedom of speech, there would be no censorship allowed on this website no matter how offensive it would be to anybody.

To ensure money, and thus corruption, stay out of the election process, political candidates would be barred from any kind of advertising outside of the central website.

Any person/organization wishing to interview any specific candidate(s), must do the same for all other candidates which are running for the same office.

The whole process would take 6 months, an outline of which is found on the next page.

Elimination Round #1
Number of candidates: 100 **Timeline:** January 1st to the end of February.

Important Dates:
 	
- January 1st
   - Randomly select 100 people as candidates for the office.
   - Website for all candidates is created and each candidate can edit their own individual page(s).
- January 31st
   - Deadline to publish education, work history, and criminal record for each candidate.
- February 28th/29th
   - Vote for 5 favorite. Top 50 voted for make it to the next round.

Elimination Round #2
Number of candidates: 50 **Timeline:** March 1st to the end of April.
Important Dates: - April 30th - Vote for 3 favorite. Top 10 voted for make it to the next round.

Elimination Round #3 (Final Round)
Number of candidates: 10 **Timeline:** May 1st to the end of June.
Important Dates: - June 30th - Vote for one person. Person with the most votes wins election.

Other requirements and/or clarifications

- If two or more candidates receive the same number of votes, and this would determine if they make it into the next round of voting, or actually win the election, some random event like picking straws, placing names in a hat, flipping a coin, etc... would take place to select the winner(s).

- The selection of the initial 100 candidates must be as random as possible and this process must be very open and public to avoid corrupting the election process.

- If, after serving one term in office, the office holder would like to be a candidate for that same office again, they would automatically be placed into the initial pool of candidates for elimination round #1. This automatic placement into the election pool could only happen one time, and must be in the election directly after their first term in office.

- You could sprinkle in some required debates and/or town hall type meetings in any of the 3 rounds of voting.

- I mentioned randomly picking 100 people, however this could be changed to 50, 200, or 1000. The number just needs to be large enough to ensure a decent pool of candidates for the people to choose from. Same thing goes for the number of people who make it to the next elimination round, the numbers 50 and 10 are just suggestions.

That's all it really takes to fix 99% of the corruption within the government of *The United States of America*.

- It guarantees that the pool of political candidates to choose from will NOT be decided by skin color, height, weight, gender, religious beliefs, financial status, etc...

- It eliminates any life long politician/king/queen and "political family dynasties".

- It frees up politicians from the need to constantly attend fund-raisers, and instead they can spend their time serving the people they represent.

- It ensures a short enough election cycle to keep voters actively engaged.

- It eliminates all the annoying political advertisements (via Internet, television, radio, mail, phone).

- It removes the need for self serving political parties.
- In summary, it guarantees that corruption is not built into the election system like it is now.

For all the Neanderthals out there who I have not yet convinced that money in the election process is corruption, here's one final analogy to prove my point. Think of a food or drink you really dislike. Now, imagine being offered $1,000,000.00 by some ad agency to appear in their ads where you would have to promote this product and attempt to get others to eat or drink it.

I would venture to guess that most of you (like myself) would take the money and promote the product even though you dislike it. There might be a few of you who would not, but the majority of humans would take the money.

Now, think about that and how it applies to our current political election process. Right now it takes millions of dollars to get elected to political office. Politicians take money from donors they may not agree with just to get elected, but once elected they have to promote the products of these large donors. This "promoting" takes the form of changing laws and regulations to benefit their wealthy donors. This has nothing to do with serving the people and everything to do with serving the rich donors. Sure doesn't seem like the government George, Thomas and Benjamin had in mind when they helped form this country!

I had written about other topics which also need to be addressed to create a better running government, but decided not to include them in this book. Until the issue of corruption in the election process is fixed, nothing else matters.

Other Bullshit:
[2] Microsoft's Hiring Practices

A perfect example of where political corruption and a wealthy person/organization get together and fuck over its citizens, is Microsoft.

In May of 2008, a few months after I had graduated from college with a B.S. in Computer Science, I decided to move to the Seattle area where tech jobs were plentiful. After being in the Seattle area for only 2 weeks, I had two separate job offers to work **AT** Microsoft, but not **FOR** Microsoft. I accepted a contract to work in their "*Windows Mobile*" division (later to be renamed "*Windows Phone*") as an SDET (Software Development Engineer in Test). I was working in a Microsoft building, on a Microsoft product and with Microsoft employees, but instead of being hired as a "Microsoft employee", I was hired as a contractor, AKA "second class disposable worker".

Microsoft contractors come in two types; "a-" and "v-" (pronounced "a dash" and "v dash"). The "a-" contractor can only work for 1 year, then Microsoft forces them take a mandatory 100 day break before they can work at Microsoft again. The "v-" contractor can in theory work forever as a 2nd class worker.

Over a span of about 6 years (June 2008 – August 2014), I worked 5 separate contracts as an SDET at Microsoft. The first 4 contracts I worked on the *Windows Phone*, and the last contract I worked on the *XBox One*. Four of these were "a-" positions, and one was a "v-". The length of employment and length of collecting unemployment benefits for these 5 contracts were:

1. Worked for 12 months, then 7 months of unemployment benefits.
2. Worked for 7 months, then 4.5 months of unemployment benefits.
3. Worked for 12 months, then 3.5 months of unemployment benefits.
4. Worked for 7 months, then 5 months of unemployment benefits.
5. Worked for 7 months, then 8.5 months of unemployment benefits.

These rough numbers total up to be:
- Employed for 45 months.
- Collected unemployment benefits for 28.5 months.

The 28.5 months on unemployment is a lot of wasted time and money for me and the State of Washington. I'm just one person though. From my own observations, approximately ¼th of all the tech people in the departments I worked in (*Windows Phone* and *XBox*) were contractors. It's just an observational guesstimate on my part, but Microsoft sure as fuck never releases this information. In-fact, when Microsoft has massive layoffs like they did in 2009 and 2014, the number of people they mention being laid off do NOT include its disposable second class contract workers. It's as if we don't really exist.

A contractor is someone you bring in to do a temporary one time job. Microsoft however, treats contractors as a flexible staff it can repeatedly hire/layoff and push onto unemployment for reasons like:

- The contractor worked for 12 months straight, let them go collect unemployment for 100 days so we don't have to treat them like a normal employee.
- Hey, version 25 of some piece of shit software is complete, let all the contractors go, even though we are planning to create version 26 of the same software. Sure, when each major software version is complete, there is a shuffling of personnel (even regular Microsoft employees). Sometimes you'll have an employee that wants to work in a different department, or maybe transfer to/from management. The end of a product cycle is the perfect time for this personnel shuffling. However, it doesn't mean you need to layoff your second class workers while you do this personnel shuffling. It's piss poor planning and leadership.

Microsoft thought I was useful enough to hire me 5 separate times as a second class worker, but for some reason they never offered me a job as a regular employee, and they also bribe government leaders via campaign contributions to increase the number of H1-B visas and thus bringing in workers all the way from India, China, and other places because they "can't find qualified workers" here in the USA.

My last contract at Microsoft was in the *XBox* department. For the 7 months leading up to the release of the *XBox One* video game console, I wrote automated tests which would help validate certain tasks a user would perform on its home screen. On launch day, when Microsoft released the *XBox One* to the world, Microsoft also unveiled a large placard in the building where I worked (Studio A). On this placard, Microsoft wrote the names of "all" the people who worked on the *XBox One*. However, Microsoft didn't include any of its 2nd class workers on this commemorative placard. Just more proof of the class system at Microsoft. In a way, working at Microsoft is sort of like the 1960's in the USA, when there were separate drinking fountains for black and white people.

This whole experience has convinced me that Microsoft actually is the "evil empire" it is sometimes jokingly referred to. Some people take a vow of silence, celibacy, or poverty. I have taken a personal vow to never purchase a single fucking thing from Microsoft ever again. I replaced their OS on my computer with a version of Linux, destroyed all my Microsoft software DVDs and their installation keys. I then tossed a few Microsoft related books into the recycle bin and even threw away my Microsoft Natural keyboard, which in my opinion will be the only thing I might miss from them. Fuck You Microsoft!

> Note: This is only my first rant against Microsoft in this book. There will be more!

Below is a picture of me in Microsoft building "Studio A" in Redmond Washington on launch day for the *XBox One* (November 2013). The placard with 1st class worker names who worked on the *XBox One* is just to my right, but out of view in the photograph.

16

Other Bullshit:

[3] Racism and Sexism from Apple's CEO

In 2014, Tim Cook, the CEO of Apple made this statement regarding the race and gender of its employees. (For the full transcript, see Appendix B.)

> "...
> Apple is committed to transparency, which is why we are publishing statistics about the race and gender makeup of our company. Let me say up front: As CEO, I'm not satisfied with the numbers on this page. They're not new to us, and we've been working hard for quite some time to improve them. We are making progress, and we're committed to being as innovative in advancing diversity as we are in developing our products.
>
> Inclusion and diversity have been a focus for me throughout my time at Apple, and they're among my top priorities as CEO. I'm proud to work alongside the many senior executives we've hired and promoted in the past few years, including Eddy Cue and Angela Ahrendts, Lisa Jackson and Denise Young-Smith. The talented leaders on my staff come from around the world, and they each bring a unique point of view based on their experience and heritage. And our board of directors is stronger than ever with the addition of Sue Wagner, who was elected in July.
> ..."

At first glance, this might not seem like racism and sexism to you, but it is! Just because he said these things eloquently and with an upbeat can-do attitude does not mean they are not racist and sexist comments.

What if someone who was not as eloquent were to present the same message, but in their own words, what would that sound like? Here's one possibility:

> "Recently in the news, there has been a lot of talk about the types of people who work in the tech industry. There have been complaints that way too many are white and/or male. While there may have been a few racist and/or sexist hiring decisions in the past, most of the reasons why you see more men working here, is there are more men pursuing degrees in Computer Science than women. Also, the reason why there are way more Asians working here than the general population of the United States represents, is that we've actively been bribing politicians to grant us H1-B visas to bring in tech workers from India and other places around Asia. This increase of foreign workers has increased the overall pool of workers we have to pick from, and has enabled us to

suppress wages.

Anyway, were not concerned at all about having too many Asians, but we are concerned about too many white men working for us.

To avoid looking bad, I've recently made some hiring decisions solely based on the fact that the applicants were women. We plan to continue this and also make other hiring decisions solely based on other superficial attributes like the pigment of your skin, who you are sexually attracted to and other stuff.

Please note that since the public has not been hounding us about age discrimination, we will continue to only look seriously at hiring young hipsters and ignore anyone with the slightest hint of wrinkles and/or gray hair.

Here at Apple, we are ready to do anything to appease the politically correct gods, regardless of what's right and wrong."

The messages are more or less the same, but how they are stated are dramatically different. **Reverse racism and reverse sexism ARE racism and sexism!**

Sure, I've singled out Apple here, but many other tech companies like Google and Microsoft have stated very similar things and they are also guilty of the same racism and sexism in their hiring process. So, what's the solution? Read the next chapter, titled "**Asking for Race, Gender and Age on Employment Application**" for a real concrete solution which will eliminate ALL racism and sexism from employment hiring decisions for every business, not just tech companies.

Other Bullshit:

[4] Asking for Race, Gender and Age on Employment Application

During the process of applying for a job, you've probably been asked the strangest questions that had absolutely nothing to do with your ability to perform the job, like:

What's your race?
What's your gender?
What's your date of birth?

Being asked these questions (regardless of their intent) is the exact opposite of the message being conveyed in this famous quote.

> "I have a dream that my four little children will one day live in a nation where they will not be judged by the color of their skin but by the content of their character".
>
> – Rev. Martin Luther King Jr.

Apparently, these questions are being asked to ensure certain quotas are met, regarding how many men/women, black/white, young/old people are hired. Wouldn't it be nice if there was a better way to ensure people are not discriminated against, without resorting to reverse-discrimination, which is discrimination itself? Here is a vastly superior solution than the one currently in use:

Solution: What we will create is the **Turing Employment Center**. This is named after Alan Turing, a famous computer scientist who came up with the concept of the *Turing Test* (among other things). The *Turing Test* is a simple concept.

- In room #1, a human types questions into a computer.
- In room #2, either a human or a computer program responds to the questions via computer.
- To pass the *Turing Test*, all that needs to occur is that the person who asked the questions thinks that a human answered them and not a machine.

All I'm doing here is taking the concept of the *Turing Test* and applying it to the job hiring process. Below is a drawing of the *Turing Employment Center* in action. In room #1, you have someone from a company, typing questions into a computer. In room #2, you have a potential employee answering the questions. The critical part about this, is that the person in room #1, who is doing the hiring, doesn't know any physical attributes of the potential employee before a hiring decision is made. This makes it impossible for them to make a hiring decision based on the color of your skin, age, gender, etc...

> Note: In this diagram and those on the following pages, I've given each stick figure a hat with the name of the type of person they represent.

Sometimes it takes more than questions and answers to determine if someone is qualified for a job. For example, it's hard to determine if someone is a good cook, can lift 25 kg, can weld steel, etc... without some sort of physical demonstration. In these cases, a 3rd room would be used, where the potential employee could demonstrate their skills.

20

The following drawings show how an employer can determine if someone who is applying for a job has the physical strength they are looking for, by showing they can lift a box weighing 25 kg onto a table.

Here we have 3 rooms, but the same basic rules apply. The person doing the hiring knows absolutely nothing about the person who is applying for the job. We start out with the employer in room #1, and the job applicant in room #2.

In this step, the employer opens a door and goes into the shared room, sets up a table and places a box on the floor.

The employer leaves the shared room, closes the door and then informs the job applicant (via computer), what task they should perform.

The person applying for the job now enters the shared room and finds the work that needs to be performed.

The job applicant performs the actual work by lifting the box onto the table.

The job applicant leaves the shared room, and notifies the employer (via computer) that the work is now complete.

The employer enters the shared room, examines the work and verifies that the person who is applying for the job did indeed have the physical strength they are looking for.

Comments on this solution:

- This would be for ALL jobs, even when someone wants to move into a different position within the company they currently work for. The key is, that the questions and tasks asked by the employer, will be good enough to find them the right employee for the new position.

- Some jobs require a specific level of education, training, and/or certification, and there should be strict verification that the person applying for the job does indeed have that education or training. You just can't put on your resume that "I'm a certified jet engine mechanic", or "I have degree in underwater basket weaving". Your education and certifications would be permanently attached to you, and using some sort of identification procedure like facial recognition, finger print, etc... the *Turing Employment Center* would be able to correctly identify you as the potential employee. This would be used to weed out fraudsters, as there are many out there who make false claims, pad their resume, or who would try to get someone else to take the employment test for them.

- It's OK for an employer to say the pay range is between $15 and $20 per hour, but the exact pay depends on how well you perform on the Turing Employment Test. It's NOT OK to set the exact pay AFTER the employer meets the new employee in person.

- An employer MUST state the pay, or pay range for a job BEFORE anyone tests for it. The old idea of "how much are you willing to work for" is bullshit. It's the employer who sets the wage. If they can't find anyone to fill the position at that wage, they have to increase it until they find someone to fill it. The concept of hiring 2 **equally qualified people** to perform similar tasks, but their pay differs on their negotiating skills is bullshit.

- In the examples I gave, I either showed a laptop computer, or just referred to "computer" in general. In practice, it would be great to have some kind of digital white-board, and possibly "speech-to-text" capabilities, to enhance the communication between the employer and the person they are interviewing.

Summary:

If we used the *Turing Employment Center* to hire EVERYONE, it would solve these problems:

- Hiring decisions based on race, gender, age, physical attractiveness, etc... would not exist.

- Pay differences would be based only on the person's skills, and nothing else.

- The ability to move up in a company would be open to everyone, and would eliminate most of the ass-kissing you see today in the workplace and also remove the ability for people to "sleep their way to the top" or otherwise be pressured into exchanging sexual favors for employment advancement, etc...

If you try to get the same awesome results the *Turing Employment Center* produces with laws or good intentions alone, **you will fail miserably** as it is literally impossible for humans to accomplish that.

Other Bullshit:

[5] The Mormon Church Claims that its Priesthood Holders can Heal People

The Mormon church, officially named "The Church of Jesus Christ of Latter-day Saints", claims that male members of its church who hold the priesthood and who are in "good standing" with church teachings and god, can literally heal people (or that god can heal through them).

The church has "13 Articles of Faith" which spell out the core beliefs of their religion. The 7th article of faith says:

> "We believe in the gift of tongues, prophecy, revelation, visions, **healing**, interpretation of tongues, and so forth."

People should have the right to believe whatever they want regarding the afterlife (if any). However, ANY claim of supernatural abilities (like healing) in THIS life, must be backed up by repeatable evidence. If a claim can't be backed up, they should be prosecuted for fraud just like any other person/organization.

I grew up in the Mormon church, attended seminary in high school, and when I turned 19 years old, I went on a mission to San Diego, California (summer of 1990 until summer of 1992) to convert others to the religion. However, instead of converting others, I converted myself (away from the church).

I was 1.5 years into the 2 year mission when I realized I no longer believed in the church. The internal social pressure however is very intense and it's a very big deal to leave the church as you're almost sure to cause conflict with the people closest to you who are still members of the church (friends, siblings, parents, spouse). At the time I was 99% sure I no longer believed in the church, but decided to stay on my mission for the remaining 6 months just in case I would change my mind later, but I did not. After returning home, I attended church a few times, then stopped going altogether. Not once over the last 27 years since then have I regretted that decision.

The point that I'm trying to make here is this: If you have some outrageous claim, you MUST be able to back it up with repeatable evidence. Examples of outrageous claims are:

1. I can fly like Superman.
2. I can climb walls like Spider-Man.
3. I can communicate with someone in another room just with my mind.
4. I can heal someone just by placing my hands on their head and saying a prayer.

If someone claimed any of the first three of these, we would consider them crazy and think they belonged in a nut house. However, since the 4th one is "religious" many in society will say... "oh that's OK, that's their religious belief and they are entitled to that". Bullshit. They are making a specific claim of super-natural abilities in THIS life. Such claims need to be backed up by repeatable evidence. If not, that person/organization should be tried in court for fraud, especially when they (like the Mormon church) require money (10% of income paid to church) to maintain these super-natural abilities.

The Mormon church does actually have many good qualities, but the core (prophets and other priesthood holders with special powers here on Earth) is a lie. Some of the positive things about the church in my opinion are:

- They are against smoking, drinking alcohol and using drugs.
- They promote a healthy lifestyle, like eating right and getting exercise.
- They discourage lying, stealing and cheating.
- They teach that you should treat others the way you want to be treated.

I don't have an issue with any of those things and try my best to do the same things myself... but so do many other people regardless of their religious beliefs. What I have a problem with is their claim that their male priesthood holders can heal people by putting some "blessed" oil on the head of a sick person, laying their hands on them and saying a prayer.

If the person gets better, they claim they healed them (or that god healed them through the priesthood holder). If the person does not get better, there are a few convenient explanations. The person was not healed because:

- ...the priesthood holder was not worthy (AKA a sinner or didn't pay 10% to the church).
- ...the priesthood holder didn't believe they could heal.
- ...the sick person didn't believe they could be healed.
- ...god had other plans.

So how do we go about proving the Mormon Prophet can't actually heal people and is thus a fraud? It's actually quite simple.

1. Gather some sick people from local hospital(s). The number of sick people needs to be fairly large (maybe 100).
2. The sickness MUST be something which DOES NOT cure itself on its own, regardless of time. It could be either non-curable, or only curable with specific medical treatment.
3. Each sick person MUST be confirmed to have the disease, and NOT have been introduced to any medicine for its treatment (from independent sources).
4. Randomly divide the sick people into 2 test groups. The Mormon Prophet will attempt to heal those in group #1. The 2nd group will be given traditional medical treatment or a placebo (fake pill that does nothing) if there is no cure for that specific illness.

If the Mormon Prophet has any healing abilities, we would expect many of the people in group #1 to be healed, but not necessarily everyone, since god may want some of them to suffer and/or die.

Just for the sake of argument, let's pretend for a minute that god definitely exists and created us humans. If this were true, don't you think this god would be really disappointed in us if we were to just blindly follow any fucking idiot who said he/she was a prophet, or some other spiritual leader, without any proof other than them saying "trust me"?

Don't be so fucking stupid. The Mormon church leaders literally claim healing powers in this life. Now is the time to call them out on their bullshit! If you're not ready to do this, for something so easily proved, what hope does humanity really have for the future?

The information I've given you to prove the Mormon church's male members, even its prophet, can't actually heal anyone, is the equivalent to the rebels in Star Wars discovering the weakness in the Death Star. The entire Mormon religion is based upon the belief that people from the afterlife visited Joseph Smith and restored the priesthood to him. This "restored priesthood" is where the Mormons get their healing powers from. If we can prove the Mormon prophet can't heal anyone, we will have proven that it's not the "one true church", and thus Joseph Smith was a con-artist.

I'm only addressing the bullshit from the Mormon religion here, because that is what I know about. I'm sure there's bullshit from other religions also, but I'll leave it up to members of those religions to figure that out and fix it.

Note to Mormons: Instead of getting mad at me for what I've said here, you should see this as a great opportunity to prove to the world how the Mormon church is indeed the one true church and that god really did restore the priesthood as Joseph Smith claimed. If the priesthood was in fact restored to Joseph Smith, your current prophet will have no problem healing the sick as described in this chapter. So, instead of getting mad at me, prove to the world that your priesthood holders actually have real healing powers. What do you have to lose? If you're right, and can prove this, your church will undoubtedly gain a lot of new members. In-fact, I would even admit I was wrong, repent of my sins and rejoin the church. However, if you're wrong, at least I helped you figure out that you were following a false prophet.

Other Bullshit:

[6] *Yahoo!* Censoring User Comments

Have you ever read an article on *Yahoo!* or some other website and noticed they provide a section for the readers to make comments about it? Well, *Yahoo!* censors what its users can say. For example, if you type "fuck", "shit", or other words THEY find offensive or not politically correct, they will either delete your post, or change the offensive word to "#$!*". This is Bull$h!t.

When I noticed this was happening, I asked *Yahoo!* why they were violating the 1st amendment to the U.S. Constitution (right to free speech), they said something to the effect that since they were a corporation, they had the right to fuck over all its users. Ha ha ha just kidding. They didn't actually say those specific words, but the meaning of what they said was exactly the same. *Yahoo!* said that their comment section was not a public place and instead on private property (their computer servers), and thus they were not violating the Constitution.

I would have to disagree with this argument. While they may own the computers, they have provided a public forum for people to talk about the article. Just because the people are not physically in the town square talking face to face does not matter, as comment sections like *Yahoo!* and others provide on the Internet IS today's version of the public town square.

One slight note should be made here: I think that it is totally OK for them to limit the scope of user comments to the current article. So, let's say someone spams their comment section with info about some get rich quick scheme, or erectile pills, when the article is on underwater basket weaving, that spam is totally fine to delete.

Other Bullshit:

[7] Santa Clause and the Tooth Fairy

OK, now you're thinking I've gone overboard on this one. What could I possibly have against Santa Clause? Well, at the root of it, we are teaching our kids that lying is OK. Is lying a "family value", I don't think so. So why would you lie to your children about Santa Clause being a real person with magical powers like knowing whose naughty and nice, visiting every home in one evening, fitting down the chimney, and flying reindeer?

Look, I was raised in a family which celebrated Christmas and was told about Santa Clause and that he brought gifts, etc... I also remember it was a lot of fun. However, eventually your kids are going to learn the truth; that is, Santa Clause is not real, and it was their parents who put the gifts under the tree. Also, the kid will realize that their parents lied to them. Kids tend to imitate their parents, and thus when your kid lies to you about something, where do you think they learned this skill from?

It's time to get rid of Santa Clause and the Tooth Fairy, or at least make sure your kids know they live in the land of make believe.

Other Bullshit:

[8] Not Using the Metric System in the U.S.A.

Here in *The United States of America*, we don't use the Metric System, and it's holding us back. For example, take a look at the differences in the unit system currently used in the U.S.A. and the Metric System for the freezing/boiling point of water:

	U.S.A. Unit System	Metric System
Water freezes at:	32 °F	0 °C
Water boils at:	212 °F	100 °C

Now think how much easier it would be for a student to remember that water freezes at 0 degrees and boils at 100, rather than at 32 and 212 degrees!

What about the weight of water given some volume?

	Volume of water	Weight of water
U.S.A. Unit System	1 cubic inch	0.036 pounds
U.S.A. Unit System	1 cubic foot	62.416 pounds
Metric System	1 cubic centimeter	1 gram
Metric System	1 cubic meter	1000 kilograms

Now we will compare the breakdown of various distances. Notice how the Metric System is based on the number 10, while the U.S.A. Unit System is random.

U.S.A. Unit System
1 mile = 5280 feet
1 foot = 12 inches
1 inch = No smaller units. Have to use fractions like ½, ¼, etc...

Metric System
1 kilometer = 1000 meters
1 meter = 100 centimeters
1 centimeter = 10 millimeters

Now let's consider volume.

U.S.A. Unit System
1 gallon = 231 cubic inches.

Metric System
1 liter = 1000 cubic centimeters.

Not only is the Metric System easier to use, it's what the scientific community uses, even here in the U.S.A.. So why the fuck are we teaching our students the shittier system of units? Because that is the way it's always been done. That's bullshit.

Other Bullshit:

[9] Internet Driven by Advertising

Many websites make some, or all of their money off of the advertisements they display on their site. This has turned the vast majority of content on the Internet into a big pile of bullshit.

The problem is not only the advertisements you see, but also to make more and more money, websites will create what are called "click-bait" pages. The sole purpose of a click-bait page is to get you to click on it! That's it. All they have to do is come up with a sensationalized picture, headline or video and get you to click on it. The actual content of the link you clicked on is totally irrelevant and is usually of poor quality.

Another despicable practice is placing Internet ads in the middle of the text you are reading, so it appears as if the ad is part of the web page text. This is absolute bullshit, and there really should be a law against it, because at its very core, is deception.

So how do we fix the Internet so it has much less bullshit? Here's a couple ideas:

Solution #1: Ban all Internet advertising. Websites will need to be funded by one of these methods:

- Self funded by owner of website.
- Funded by donations (like Wikipedia).

The problem with solution #1, is that I'm sure some website owner would claim that banning advertising would infringe on their right to free speech. For normal ads, they would probably be correct. However, those deceptive ads which appear to be part of the article you are reading should still be considered fraudulent and be against the law.

Solution #2: Only allow a single, well defined advertisement per website. No click-bait, no in-line deception, but a clearly marked area that is for the advertisement. If the user clicks on multiple pages on that site, they ONLY see that one ad, not one per page.

This could be verified by an independent monitor, and websites that adhere to this standard, could get a "seal of approval".

Other Bullshit:

[10] Appending Changes to the U.S. Constitution, Instead of Modifying it

Since 1789, the Constitution of the United States has been amended 27 times. Little changes like letting women vote, ending slavery, giving people the right to speak their mind without fear of being thrown in jail, etc...

However, for some idiotic reason, all changes to the U.S. Constitution are just added on to the end, instead of being modified in-line, and this creates a document which has contradictory statements in it and is hard for the average citizen to get a clear understanding of what is in the Constitution and what is not. This is bullshit.

Here's a simple analogy of the problem. Let's say you have a list of things you need to buy at the store next time you go there. You start the list with:

Grocery List
- Apples
- Bananas
- Soup

This is a simple and easy to understand list. However, sometime later you decide to add "Bread" and remove "Apples" from the list. If we were to change the grocery list like the U.S. Constitution is changed, it would look like this:

Grocery List
- Apples
- Bananas
- Soup
- Bread
- Don't buy apples.

You have both "Apples" and "Don't buy apples" on the list. This very simple example is fucked up, now imagine changing the grocery list 27 times like the U.S. Constitution has been and imagine how hard it would be to know what you need to get at the store.

What the modified grocery list should look like is:

Grocery List

- Bananas
- Soup
- Bread

As far as I can tell, there isn't a "current view" of the Constitution, just all of this bullshit of adding changes to the end, and not removing the old words/sentences/paragraphs. **This is the core document describing how our country is to operate**, yet I have no idea what EXACTLY is in and out of the document. This is beyond fucked up.

A much better way to organize all the information in the Constitution would be to write it down in an electronic document like you see below where its organized into different sections with each section having a title for what will be contained in it.

US Constitution

1. **Branches of government.**

    <Insert existing info here>

2. **Election process.**

    <Insert new election process here>

3. **Individual rights.**

    <Insert existing info here>

4. **Etc...**

Once you have all the current Constitution data re-organized into this new electronic document, add it to a "version control" software system. This lets people see what the current version of the document is, as well as any previous versions, as well as what specific changes were made between each version.

Any changes you make, would be done in the section in which it applied to, and not just added on to the end.

Other Bullshit:

[11] Employment Contract that said I Couldn't Say Anything Bad About Company

One of the contracting companies I "worked for" while at Microsoft, was *Insight Global*. I put "worked for" in quotes, because I really didn't work for them at all in my opinion. The only thing they did was pass my resume to Microsoft as a potential 2nd class worker. When Microsoft was interested in me, Microsoft would tell the contracting company to inform me to show up at a Microsoft building, where Microsoft employees would interview me for the contract job.

Once hired, the only thing the contracting company did was take a cut of every paycheck I received. So, in a very real way, contracting companies at Microsoft, like *Insight Global*, are literal parasites that live off the hard work of the people doing the actual work.

Not only that, but *Insight Global* actually attempts through "legal" means to intimidate its workers into keeping their fucking mouths shut if they disliked working for them. Below is clause #17 of an employment contract I had to sign with *Insight Global* when I worked on the Microsoft *XBox One* in 2013. The highlighted section is what I'm most concerned with. (The "Customer" is Microsoft.)

> 17. **Non-Disparagement**. Contract Employee agrees that during his/her employment with *Insight Global*, Contract Employee will abide by all *Insight Global* and Customer policies regarding employee communications. Following the termination of Contract Employee's employment for any reason, Contract Employee further agrees that he/she will not make any derogatory or disparaging statement about *Insight Global*, Customer, or any of their products or services, employees, consultants, officers, directors, or shareholders, or any of them, nor directly or indirectly take any action which is intended to embarrass any of them.

To me, and I'm not a lawyer, this says that if someone asks how I liked working for *Insight Global*, I am legally bound to not say anything negative at all. Hey, *Insight Global*, FUCK YOU and your intimidation tactics.

Bullshit like this is EXACTLY why we have the 1st amendment to the Constitution. The first amendment is designed to protect the little guy from this kind of censorship and intimidation. In case *Insight Global* forgot what the first amendment says, here it is, and remember, this is **THE SUPREME FUCKING LAW OF THE LAND!**

> Amendment I
>
> **Congress shall make no law** respecting an establishment of religion, or prohibiting the free exercise thereof; or **abridging the freedom of speech**, or of the press; or the right of the people peaceably to assemble, and to petition the Government for a redress of grievances.

Note: Some really simple minded primates right now are thinking that I don't understand the first amendment, and that it does not apply to corporations. Let me correct your illogical reasoning.

Fact: Congress makes the laws.

Fact: Congress can't make a law, which takes away "free speech".

Fact: A corporation, gets it's ability to create contracts with it's employees, **from the laws** that Congress created.

Fact: This contract is a direct descendant of a law passed by Congress.

What *Insight Global* and the scum sucking lawyer(s) who wrote this up need to understand, there is a difference between making a false claim against them and simply stating an opinion of how I liked or disliked working for them. This "legal" contract went too far and was taking away my right to state my opinion of the company and how it treats its employees. If asked, I should be able to tell someone that I liked or disliked working for them and why. Maybe they are the greatest place to work, or complete slave drivers. Either way, you can't take away my 1st amendment rights.

Making a false claim is something completely different and if you read the chapter on the Mormon Church and how they make false claims of super-natural abilities you will know how I feel about that.

For the record, I found *Insight Global* to be less of a parasite than *Volt Technical Services*, the other contracting company I "worked for" while working on Microsoft products, in Microsoft buildings with Microsoft employees.

While I'm on the subject of *Insight Global's* employment contract, I'd like to take the time to point out one other case of bullshit. Here is part of clause #14 of the document I had to sign.

14. **Employment with Customer.**

… Contact Employee understands that he/she is not allowed to leave the employment of *Insight Global* to work for another staffing agency for Customer for a period of 180 days subsequent to Contract Employee's termination of employment with *Insight Global*.

> Note: I had to sign something similar with *Volt Technical Services* when they were my parasitic contracting company while I worked at Microsoft.

Let's document how many things are wrong with clause #14. First of all, it contradicts itself. It says "…is not allowed to leave the employment of *Insight Global*…180 days subsequent to Contract Employee's termination of employment with *Insight Global*." How could I leave your employment if I no longer work for you?

The contradiction is just poor writing. What they are trying to say here is that after my contract ends at Microsoft, I can't return to work at Microsoft as a contractor for 180 days (6 months) …**IF**… I use some other parasitic contracting company.

This 180 day waiting period to switch to a different contract company is totally separate from the mandatory 100 days off Microsoft requires to ensure its 2nd class workers are treated as such (see the chapter on "Microsoft's Hiring Practices"). So, after your "a-" contract ends you MUST take 100 days off from working at Microsoft. Once those 100 days are up, you are free to return as a 2nd class worker using the SAME parasitic contacting company, but if you want to switch to a different parasitic contracting company you must wait 80 more days to do that.

Why does the 180 day waiting period even exist? The contracting company does not build or create anything itself, all it's doing is sucking money out of each of my paychecks. I guess it's just trying to protect its own turf. It's just another example of bullshit the American worker has to deal with.

Also, after talking with other contractors about this mandatory break before I could switch parasitic contracting companies, many were under the impression that this would not hold up in a court of law in the State of Washington. The consensus seemed to be that I'd need to waste my own money consulting with a lawyer to figure out if this was legally binding or not.

This is starting to smell like that special kind of bullshit... you know the "corruptocracy" kind! Microsoft bribes politicians with "campaign contributions". One of the things it gets in return is the ability to maintain a shit load of 2nd class workers (AKA contractors) instead of them being "normal" employees. To keep the 2nd class workers in-line and from trying to find a better parasitic contracting company, Microsoft and the parasite place unreasonable waiting periods on the contractors, knowing full well that most people can't hold out that long without employment and will thus be forced to deal with the same parasitic contracting company over and over again.

The corrupt politicians who took the Microsoft bribes are not going to say anything bad about Microsoft, so instead of the politicians doing their jobs and sticking up for workers rights, they do nothing and once again it's the worker who gets screwed over.

Other Bullshit:

[12] Unable to Remove Crapware from Computing Devices

Another prime example of how corruptocracy screws you over is in the lack of consumer protection. Over the last few years, I've purchased the following items, and got screwed over with each one:

1. HP desktop computer.
2. Microsoft *Surface RT* tablet.
3. Samsung *Galaxy S4* Android phone.

HP desktop computer

A number of years ago I was in the market for a new desktop computer. Instead of building it myself, I got lazy and decided to just buy one that was already assembled. After searching around, I found an HP desktop which satisfied my needs. However, when the computer was shipped to me, I was pissed off beyond words. HP said the computer would be running the "*Windows 7*" Operating System (the latest OS from Microsoft at the time). However, the OS they had on the computer was NOT "*Windows 7*", it was "*Windows 7* plus a bunch of HP crapware".

At first I tried to un-install this crapware, but soon realized it was virtually impossible to get rid of everything. The OS disks they sent with the computer were NOT a "clean" version of "*Windows 7*" either. A re-install of the OS using those disks put the HP crapware back on the computer, and there wasn't any option during installation of the operating system NOT to install that HP crapware.

The only option I had was to use a "real *Windows 7*" disk (purchased separately), and that is what I did. The computer hardware ran just fine with that "clean" version of the OS and it obviously didn't need the extra HP crapware to work properly.

My main issue with the HP desktop computer is they said it came with the "*Windows 7*" OS. It did not. If they had said, it comes with a "Frankenstein version of *Windows 7*, with crapware", I NEVER would have bought it.

Microsoft *Surface RT* tablet

When Microsoft released its first version of the *Surface RT* tablet I was intrigued, and since I didn't have a portable computer I decided to buy it. Turns out that purchase was a waste of money. About the only thing I found the device useful for, was streaming an extremely poor selection of movies from Netflix.

After my divorce from all things Microsoft (see earlier chapter on "Microsoft's Hiring Practices"), I knew I needed to either install a version of Linux on the device, sell it, or throw it away. However, with the *Surface RT*, Microsoft made it impossible (via "secure boot") to install any other Operating System on it other than *Windows*.

I had given Microsoft money, and they gave me computer hardware which just happened to be running a version of their OS. As a consumer, I have every right to install any fucking OS I want on it (assuming compatibility). As a super-big-international-corporation-who-pays-off-politicians-with-bribes-aka-campaign-contributions, Microsoft knows they have little to fear from the little guy so they introduce this "secure boot" as a way to crush other Operating Systems. It's apparently required on all *Windows 8* devices, but only on the *Surface RT* tablet is the user NOT able to disable "secure boot" and install any OS they want.

My guess is that Microsoft wants all computers in the future which are sold with *Windows*, to be as restrictive as the *Surface RT* tablet currently is, but figured they would use the *Surface RT* tablet as a trail to see how much shit they caught for this stunt. If nobody complains too much, they will most likely require all future computers sold with *Windows* to be unable to install any other OS on it. This is major league bullshit, not to mention a complete lack of confidence that consumers will actually like their OS.

Samsung *Galaxy S4* Android phone

On Thanksgiving weekend of 2013, I was in the market for a new phone. Not that I really needed a new phone, but being in the tech industry, I figured I didn't want to look like a dinosaur and get caught carrying around a 2 year old phone (I hate succumbing to peer pressure).

As far as "smart phones" go, I had owned 2 previous; a *Windows Mobile 6.1* device, and an *iPhone 4s*. Since Android phones were real popular at the time, I figured I would try one out, after all Android is supposedly running a version of Linux and I use a Linux based OS on my computer at home, so my gut told me it would be a good fit. What could possibly go wrong?

The first issue I had, was that I was losing text messages. On my previous *iPhone*, I had been using "*iMessage*" to text with other *iPhone* users. Now, for some reason, I could send a text using my Android phone to an *iPhone* user I had previously communicated with via *iMessage*, but when they replied, I would not get the reply. This is data loss, and absolute bullshit!

For example, let's say Alice and Bob are in a relationship. Both had *iPhones* and were using *iMessage* to text each other. Then Bob gets a different phone, which is not from Apple, and thus does not have *iMessage* capability.

Bob then sends a normal SMS text to Alice, saying "I love you". Alice receives the text, and replies, "I love you too". However, Alice's *iPhone* is not "smart" and sends the text via *iMessage* and since Bob no longer has an *iPhone*, he never gets the reply and assumes Alice no longer cares for him and they break up.

I hope you can see how this data loss can be very bad... think of the impact of missing texts from work, friends, family could have on your life. I contacted Apple about this, and they knew full well about the bug and they told me I'd have to contact everyone I had previously used *iMessage* with and inform them to make sure to explicitly change my contact to send text messages as SMS and NOT *iMessage*. Fuck you Apple. This bug is very fixable. What you do is shut down *iMessage* and force all text messages through SMS until you pull your head out of your ass and fix the problem.

OK, that was the first issue and really had nothing to do with the shitty Samsung phone I had purchased, as the Apple bug would have been hit if I had purchased any non-Apple phone.

Back to the shitty Samsung *Galaxy S4*. I had heard how "open" the Android platform was and that it was extremely customizable, blah blah blah. One of the first things I noticed (other than the Apple *iMessage* bug), was that the Samsung phone had a lot of apps on it which I could not remove. One of these un-installable apps was *DropBox*.

If you read about my experience with HP and their crapware, you will not be surprised that I wanted to un-install apps on the phone I would not be using. However, Google and/or Samsung decided to fuck over its customers and not allow certain apps to be un-installed. All un-installable apps which have nothing to do with the functionality of the OS instantly become crapware in my opinion.

I have no problem with Samsung and/or Google saying, "hey, here's some apps we think you will like", but not "hey, here's some apps that paid us some money and we will never let you un-install them". Also, letting us "disable" the app is NOT the same as un-installing it.

Apparently, to get around the un-installable app issue you have to "root" the phone. This sounds like it would require some crazy high tech super nerd capabilities, but in Linux based operating systems, which Android is, "root" simply means "system administer", instead of "normal user". Every Linux computer I've ever owned (except this phone) lets me access "root" when needed, but as recommended, you typically only use "root" for very specific configuration issues, not for day-to-day tasks.

What Google and/or Samsung have done is say, we don't trust you to be the "system administrator", so they took it away.

If the phone had not pissed me off enough, there was another shitty thing about it. I purchased it while living in Washington State and was using T-Mobile service. About the only thing cool about the phone, was I could make phone calls via Wi-Fi, when I had no cellular service. This feature was built into the phone and was NOT some 3rd party app. This Wi-Fi calling capability came in real handy on a trip to the Big Island of Hawaii in February of 2014. The place I was staying didn't have cell coverage, but did have Wi-Fi Internet. I was able to still make and receive phone calls even though there was no cell reception.

However, later that year when I moved from Washington to Alaska (late August of 2014), I found out T-Mobile didn't have any cell towers in Alaska, and I'd have to switch to AT&T. All I did was go into the AT&T store and they gave me an AT&T SIM card for the phone, and I was now able to use the same exact phone on AT&T cell towers. But... for some reason AT&T does not allow Wi-Fi calling on the same exact fucking phone. My only guess to why this would be, is that AT&T sees Wi-Fi calling as a threat to their "business model".

And lastly the updates, or should I say lack thereof. The apps on the phone would get regular updates, but the core OS stopped getting updated after about 2.5 years (if I recall correctly). It could have been maybe a little longer, but I remember it was a very short period of time in which Samsung actually gave a crap about the device. Any device which stops receiving regular OS updates is NOT SECURE. At the bare minimum, they should state on the cover of the device IN BOLD LETTERS, how long they will support it, and then release the firmware source code when they stop supporting it, so others can take over this responsibility.

So there you have it. I buy this Android phone and it loses some, but not all of my text messages. It has crapware apps which I can't un-install. Using the same phone on AT&T instead of T-Mobile disables the only cool feature of the damn phone. The device stopped receiving OS updates after about 2.5 years. What can I say, other than this phone has been bullshit from day one.

Other Bullshit:

[13] Junk Mail

While I was writing the first version of this book, a postal worker delivered to me a piece of junk mail. The mail was in the form of a postcard, and I've scanned both the front and back of it for you to read.

*** Front side of postcard. ***

*** Back side of postcard. ***

VERY URGENT AND TIME SENSITIVE

YOUR MANUFACTURERS WARRANTY MAY BE ABOUT TO EXPIRE OR HAS RECENTLY EXPIRED BASED ON AGE OR MILEAGE.

DEADLINE: 12/02/2014

ATTENTION ISAAC POWELL,

This is a very URGENT notice to inform you that the factory warranty on your 2010-SUBARU vehicle that you purchased has expired or is about to expire. **Please contact us IMMEDIATELY**; as this notice will expire by the **deadline date**. Please call us as soon as possible to see what your options are to extend coverage. If you go without coverage, you will be responsible for all repairs in the event of a breakdown. If you do not contact us by the deadline date, you risk not being able to extend coverage.

Please Call
(███) ███-████

Monday through Friday 8:00 a.m. - 7:00 p.m. CST
Saturday 10:00 a.m. - 2:00 p.m. CST

25059

This junk mail was sent to my address, identified me as the owner of a 2010 Subaru, and the fact that since my car was 4.5 years old, its warranty had expired. All of that was correct. However, in my opinion, it's very deceptive.

I expect that anything mailed to me with **"VEHICLE ALERT NOTICE"** in all red caps and correctly identifies me and the car I drive, to be something important. I would expect those words to be used if my car had some urgent safety recall from the car's manufacture, not some bullshit ad for some company trying to sell me an extended warranty on my vehicle.

Sure, I was able to determine this junk mail was bullshit, but why should we be subjected to this? This is another prime example of corruptocracy in action, where those in charge would rather line their pockets with bribes than put a quick end to these deceptive tactics, which obviously work on some people (probably the elderly) or they would not be sent.

Junk mail is not always deceptive though, sometimes the sender is upfront with what they are trying to push on you, either way, it's all bullshit. In my previous apartment in Redmond Washington, all the mail boxes were in one central location, and the property owner set out a huge recycle bin for people to put their junk mail directly into.

Do you have any idea how much of an epic waste of resources it is to produce and send all that junk mail, just to have it thrown directly into the trash? It wastes paper, ink, fuel to transport it, our time, and most of all people don't want it (at least people with more than 3 functioning brain cells).

Here's my challenge to the dip-shits in Washington D.C.. Next election cycle, give the voters a chance to vote on whether they want one of these to occur:

1. All junk mail to be banned.
2. Opt-in requirement to receive junk mail.
3. Opt-out option to stop receiving junk mail.

So, let's pretend this situation actually occurs and the people actually get to vote on this, or the politicians just implement it without the people voting on it. The big question is: Would this change be a result of democracy? The answer is no!

If we had a democracy, the politicians in charge would have put an end to this bullshit many years ago, as junk mail has long been despised by almost everyone.

This would be an example of one of those situations I mentioned in the first chapter where even kings/queens know to backtrack when the people are overwhelmingly against them, and it has nothing to do with democracy, as those assholes in Washington D.C. and also in your state capital, don't represent you or me, but rather the people who line their pockets with cash.

Other Bullshit:

[14] Safeway Club Card

One day back in 2002, I walked into a Safeway grocery store to buy some food. During the checkout process, I had a conversation with the cashier that went something like this:

Safeway Cashier:	Do you have a Safeway Club Card?
Me:	No, what is it?
Safeway Cashier:	It's a little plastic card that saves you money on every purchase.
Me:	How much does it cost?
Safeway Cashier:	Nothing, it's free.
Me:	So let me get this straight. If you give me this free plastic card, I can save money on every purchase I make, but if I don't have this free plastic card, I don't save any money?
Safeway Cashier:	Yes, that's correct.
Me:	What do I have to do to get this card?
Safeway Cashier:	Just give us your name, address, and phone number.
Me:	Isn't that the same as saying, people who don't give you their personal information and let you track every purchase they make, have to pay more for their food, which is one of the basic needs for survival?
Safeway Cashier:	<silent>
Me:	That's bullshit!

This is another perfect example of corruptocracy in action. No government which actually represented the people would allow a large powerful corporation like Safeway, whose primary business is to sell food (one of the core things that keeps you alive besides clean water/air and shelter), to force you into letting them track every food purchase you make.

I'm sure some people at Safeway (lawyer, CEO, and/or board members) do not think of this as "forcing" someone to use their club card, but they don't fucking get it. The cost of food for normal folks is a very important part of their budget. They just don't have the option to pay more for their food to avoid having Safeway track all of their purchases.

Safeway is not the only mega-corporation which does this, and it seems like almost every time I go into any store, I'm asked if I have that store's special card. Fuck you Safeway, and all the other stores who hike up prices for people who don't want to be cyber-stalked.

Other Bullshit:

[15] The "Reboot" of Star Trek

> Pre-Chapter Note: I've left this chapter as it was written in 2015. At the end of the chapter, I will have some post-chapter comments about recent developments.

Star Trek began as a television show in 1966. While the original series only ran for 3 seasons, it has spawned many movies in addition to other Star Trek television series like:

- Star Trek: The Next Generation   // Ran for 7 seasons.
- Star Trek: Voyager   // Ran for 7 seasons.
- Star Trek: Enterprise   // Ran for 4 seasons.
- Star Trek: Deep Space Nine   // Ran for 7 seasons.

You don't get to produce 28 seasons of Star Trek without having a solid fan base. However, recently someone came up with a really bad idea. They thought it would be great to find actors which looked like the actors from the original Star Trek in 1966, tweak the timeline a little bit, then have these look-alike and sound-alike actors retell some of the same stories from the original series.

Basically, they wanted to make a new Star Trek movie, but could not think up any new ideas of their own, so instead, they came up with this reboot idea, which to be completely honest would make a great *Saturday Night Live* comedy skit, but is absolutely devastating to the fan base who deserve new content, not rehashed stories from look-alike and sound-alike actors. This is bullshit.

> Note: This is not meant to be criticism of the actors of the reboot, but rather of the people who produce, direct, wrote, or in anyway gave the green light for it to be made.

To fix this will require a two part plan.

1. Come up with a way to restore the original timeline.
2. Find people who are not brain dead and who also have at least a tiny bit of creativity come up with a new Star Trek television series.

There are a few possible solutions for restoring the timeline back to what it was.

- In the first episode of the newly created Star Trek television series, have "Q", who is almighty, all-knowing, etc... say that the new timeline was boring, and his favorite human, Jean-Luc Picard, was missing from it, and thus have "Q" fix it by snapping his fingers.
- Come up with some story about how the Starfleet time ship *Relativity* (seen a few times in the Star Trek Voyager series) was somehow not affected by the timeline changes because it was in an earlier time when the actual timeline was changed (or something similar). Then explain that the crew of the ship *Relativity* had been busy tracing down the exact cause of the timeline disruption, and then have members of that spaceship fix the timeline.
- Build a real time machine, go back a few years and convince the movie producers never to reboot the series. I'm pretty sure this is the most difficult one to accomplish.

After the Star Trek timeline has been restored, what's next? Star Trek has historically been structured as a television series, which if done well enough and the storyline permits, to then make a few movies using the characters from that television series. I would recommend returning to this format, instead of just making movies.

Once you decide to make a new Star Trek television series, anything is possible, as this is science fiction after all. I would recommend the star-date in which this new series take place, to occur AFTER all the other existing Star Trek television series have already taken place, this way you're completely open to new stories, and if you want to bring in one of the characters from a previous series, the actor will have aged in real life to fit the new star-date. However, please don't rely too much, if at all, on bringing back the glory days of previous Star Trek actors, as while they did a great job, most of their back story is already known, and little is left for character development.

Star Trek Voyager could be a source of inspiration for new ideas, as it took members of Star Fleet out from its local neighborhood and introduced other species and whatnot. Maybe the new series could use some new technology which allows Starfleet to venture off to remote parts of the galaxy, or god forbid, out of the Milky Way Galaxy altogether.

You could even bring in another android creation of Dr. Noonien Soong, as Lt. Commander Data was not the only one he created. Maybe this android could be the actual creation of Dr. Soong, or maybe of some other brilliant scientist who was able to expand upon his work.

The possibilities of what you can do in a new, clean, Star Trek series are endless, and it's what the Star Trek fans deserve.

One final personal request: Please, for the love of god, don't make another series based upon the life around a space station like "Deep Space Nine". I was able to eat up everything from all the other series and loved them, but could not for the life of me finish even season #1 of Deep Space Nine, and I gave it a few good attempts to get excited about it, however it never caught my imagination. I guess I'm just more interested in spaceships flying around and exploration, than the boring life around a space station.

Post-Chapter Notes: Star Trek is dying!

The main reason, is the dual ownership between Viacom and CBS. This has forced VERY bad decisions to be made, which turned "Star Trek" into "Franken Trek".

Due to severe financial issues, I have not been able to view any of these new shows that call themselves "Star Trek", but I've read enough from people I trust, to know that things are not good.

The secondary reason for suckage, is the social disease floating around Hollywood, which states your genitals, the color of your skin, etc… are what's important in making a good show. WRONG. To make a good show, you start with good writing. After that, you need good writing, and a little more good writing. Then add in some special effects, sound, etc…

Recommendation: Let Star Trek die. Move on, find new shows to watch, or pick up a useful hobby like "underwater basket weaving", anything but waste your time on this crap.

Other Bullshit:

[16] Religion vs. Atheism

In general, there seems to be two types of people in the world: Religious and Atheist. These two groups argue all the time about which one is right. I'm going to resolve this stupid debate once and for all.

...and the answer is: Neither of them are correct.

If you're an atheist, you claim to know that god does NOT exist, and you've accepted the Theory of Evolution and the Big Bang. If you're religious, you believe in one or more gods, which created you, or at least created the first few humans, and after many generations, here you are.

The problem with both religious and atheist people, is that they claim to **know for a fact** how we came into existence and don't consider other possibilities.

The religious folks tend to rely on old books, which they claim to be written by god, or at least by humans who were close to god in one way or another. Some problems with this are:

- Which book is the right one? Bible, Quran, Torah, Harry Potter, Book of Mormon, etc...
- How do you know the book was not written as a work of fiction? That is, way back in the day, I'm pretty sure people enjoyed a good story now and then, even if it was not totally true.
- If the book was supposedly true, how do you know the person(s) writing it were not completely full of shit? Humans lie all the time (some more than others). Coming up with a story to convince people to give you 10% of their income seems like a scam to me.

The atheist crowd doesn't blindly follow anything, and relies upon observing how the universe seems to work, then draws conclusions based upon this. Personally, this methodical analysis and not blindly trusting other humans is appealing to me, but the key problem is they claim that god does not exist. **That is not provable!** Sure, atheists can point to fraudsters like the Mormon prophet who claims to have actual healing powers (when he doesn't) and infer that because the Mormon prophet is full of shit, all other religious leaders are also, and thus because the Mormon god does not exist, NO god can exist, but this is faulty logic.

So what are some other possibilities for how we came into existence?

- Maybe god does exist, and this god created the big bang? In this reality, god creates specific creatures (dogs, cats, humans, etc...) and over time, those creatures with the best genes survive and pass their genes on, however this "evolution" of a species starts off with fully formed creatures, not from scratch.
- Maybe the entire universe is simply a computer simulation.
- Maybe YOU are the computer simulation, and parts of the world/universe are just rendered when needed, since trying to render the entire universe all at once might take up too many computing resources.
- Maybe some other advanced species has a need for punishing those who do wrong, but instead of sticking them in a cage (like humans do), they plug them into this existence (think The Matrix and/or Total Recall movies) for as long as their punishment is to last.
- On the flip side of the virtual prison idea, maybe this advanced species is all knowing and are looking for an escape from their reality and this life is their vacation.

  Along this idea, maybe they're able to plug into other creatures besides humans. This could explain the dinosaur extinction. Maybe being plugged into the "dinosaur experience" was real popular for awhile, but once the Neanderthals came along, they became the new rage and a superior experience and since fewer and fewer of these advanced species were signing up for the "dinosaur experience", they became extinct. Then version 2.0 of the Neanderthals came along (AKA Humans), and maybe the "human experience" was vastly superior, and thus the Neanderthals were "retired".

- Ever have a near death experience? Well, maybe you actually did die, but just like those old video arcade games where you had the option to insert more quarters to continue playing, maybe the "person" playing you, inserted more credits into their video game to continue playing you. Once the credits were inserted, time was re-started 1-2 seconds before you died, but this time you live, and you mark it up as a "close call" or "brush with death".
- Try watching Star Trek: The Next Generation: Season 5, Episode 25 "The Inner Light". This is one of my favorite episodes of the series.

If you use your imagination, you might think of a few more possibilities for how we came into existence. The point is, you just can't know for certain if god exists or not. Just because you observe evolution in various species, doesn't mean god didn't create the first few, then let genetics take over and letting those with the best genes survive.

Also, just because your parents or other adults in your life told you that there's a god living in the clouds and that this supreme, all knowing, all powerful god needs money and good behavior or else you'll be punished, does NOT make it true. It just means they didn't have any better way to get you to behave like they wanted, so they used this god to get the results they were looking for.

So, if the answer to how we came into existence is NOT found in religion or atheism, what is the answer? **Agnostic** is the answer. Basically it refers to people who have accepted the fact that KNOWING the truth about god's existence is NOT possible. They have accepted the fact that maybe god does or does not exist, but make no definitive claim one way or the other.

Just because god does not hang out with us in the literal physical sense, does not mean god does not exist, as it very well could be that god intentionally does not show proof that he/she/it exists, because this god wants to see how we behave without this proof. And on the flip side, I've never seen in all my days any single fucking human with super-natural abilities (regardless of their religious title) but I have seen a lot of bullshit.

I think that maybe what religious people possibly get hung up on, is that they are told things like "treat others the way you want to be treated", "don't steal", "don't kill", and "don't fuck your neighbor's wife". Things like that make sense to a lot of people, although there are some exceptions. So, the religious person gets attached to these rules, then along comes an atheist, who says there is no god. Then the faulty logic in their brain tells them that "if there is no god", that also means that all their rules, like "don't steal" are also false, but that is not necessarily true. It is totally possible that their god does NOT exist AND it is also wrong to steal.

The atheist probably gets hung up on the fact that they see a human dressed up as a religious leader, and preaching stuff out of an old book and pretending to be best friends with god and all that. The atheist is able to see through that bullshit and realize these people are just actors who are good at manipulating other humans, usually to get money from their pockets. Their brain then tells them that these religious leaders don't have any special abilities and are more or less con-artists. They then determine that since these religious leaders are full of shit, their god does not exist either. It could be true that the religious fraudster's god probably does not exist, but that says nothing about SOME god possibly existing.

If you're an atheist and are absolutely convinced of the Theory of Evolution, think about this idea: As a computer programmer I know that whenever possible, I reuse existing computer code. So, if I were to write two separate computer programs that were to simulate a Human and also an Ape, there is a good chance the actual computer code would be very similar between the two. If you were to break down the computer programs for both the simulated Human and simulated Ape down to binary level, so you only saw the 1's and 0's, then compared how much of their computer code was similar, you may find the same high levels of similar computer code as you would if you were to compare the DNA of the actual creatures. DNA, can be thought of as computer code with an alphabet of 4, instead of 2, which our computer programs have. Just something to think about next time you make a big deal out of how similar our DNA is when compared to some other creature.

It is OK to admit you don't know something, and the age old question of "does god exist" is no different. You can ponder the idea and come up with various reasons for why, or why not, the only problem is you **can't** state for a fact that you know the answer to this question without proof... and an old book, pretty sunset, funny feeling inside are NOT proof. Proof of god's existence only comes when he/she/it gets off their lazy ass and comes down to our level and demonstrates their "almightiness" in person and NOT through some human claiming god spoke to them.

A word of warning... There have been multiple episodes of Star Trek, where a warp capable species visited a planet which was not as advanced, and the less advanced species (like us) treated the new visitors as god(s). Don't fall for this trick!

Other Bullshit:

[17] "Single Use" Batteries

Batteries come in two types:

1. Single use. You use these once, then throw them away.
2. Rechargeable. You use it, recharge it, use it again, over and over again.

When I was a little kid, back in the 1970's, I remember trying out rechargeable batteries for some toy I had received for Christmas. I was very disappointed in the power coming out of the rechargeable batteries, as they just didn't seem to be anything close to what a normal *single use* battery could provide. I would not buy any more rechargeable batteries for a few decades because of this experience.

In 2011, when I first got interested in simple "line following" robots, I decided to try out rechargeable batteries again, as supposedly they had made vast improvements over all those years. While someone might be able to point to some statistics somewhere about how well product x performs using a *single use* battery, vs. rechargeable, their performance was plenty good for me and I decided to go all out and only use rechargeable batteries in all my electronics from then on.

So why are *single use* batteries bullshit?

- Their performance advantage is no longer that big (if any) when compared to rechargeables.

- Sealed inside each battery are chemicals, which are used to store the electricity the battery provides. What impact on the environment do you think using 1000 *single use* batteries has, vs. a single rechargeable which you reuse 1000 times? The companies which still produce and sell *single use* batteries, like Duracell, are putting money before environment, when there is no need to do so.

An example of how stupid it is to still be manufacturing and selling *single use* batteries are cell phones. How would you feel if every time your cell phone ran low on its charge, you had to replace the batteries inside it? That would be fucking stupid, and you know that. The same rechargeable battery technology in your cell phone is available in other form factors like "AA", "AAA", "D",

"9v", etc... It's just that companies like Duracell know they can make more money by selling dumb fucks new batteries each time theirs runs low.

Once again, if we had a government which was not bought and paid for, maybe they would be sticking up for us and not allowing corporate greed to contaminate our environment unnecessarily, especially when there are better solutions available right now.

Other Bullshit:

[18] The Internet Being Hailed as One of the Greatest Inventions of All Time

Different generations have seen various inventions affect their lives. During my life, which spans more than 48 years so far, it would be hard to name a single invention which has had more of an impact on how the world works than the Internet.

Using the Internet, we're able to send and receive information (and disinformation) around the world more or less instantly. People who have access to the Internet have used it to replace newspapers, physical trips to the bank, sending letters via the post office, and even going to the movie theater. Many hail this as one of the greatest inventions of all time, ranking up there with fire, the wheel, or the light bulb. That is bullshit.

> Note: I do vaguely realize there is a difference between the "Internet" and the "World Wide Web", but the general public uses the term "Internet" to refer to both, so I am doing the same thing here. I'm talking about the whole process of connecting two or more computers together, transferring data between them, then possibly displaying that data.

Sure, the Internet has been very disruptive to existing industries and does serve a useful purpose, but it is NOT even close to being one of the greatest inventions of all time. To figure out the importance of an invention, you need to compare it with some other invention.

Here's a list of inventions, I think are greater than the Internet (in no particular order).

- Control of fire
- The wheel
- Light bulb
- Discovery and control of electricity.
- Automobile
- Airplane

- Washer machine
- Clothes dryer (Not everyone lives in dry warm climates where they can just use the sun.)
- Telephone
- Computer (Yes, they can be used without the Internet)
- Soap
- Glass
- Corrective lenses (to fix your vision).
- Sewing machine
- Radio
- Television
- Tooth brush
- Pen / Pencil
- Paper
- X-ray Machine
- Telescope
- Microscope
- Shoes
- Clothes (shirts, pants, socks, etc...)
- Camera
- Motion pictures (AKA Movies)
- Refrigerator / Freezer
- Indoor pluming
- Being able to control the heating in a building, by turning a knob, as apposed to having to build a fire for heat. If you don't think this is a big deal, see how bad you smell after sitting by a fire all day long.
- Air-conditioning

I'm sure there are others, but I'll stop there. Now, let's pretend that you're presented a choice by some all knowing, all powerful being, like god, or "Q" from Star Trek. The choice is this: Tomorrow, either the Internet, or one of these other inventions I've listed will be erased from existence and you will never get to use that technology ever again (or even to re-invent it). Now, how important is the Internet really? Would you be willing to wash and dry your clothes by hand, revert to using a horse to getting around, what about never being able to listen to the radio, or having to build a fire every time you got cold?

We think the Internet is such a big deal, and sure it has had a big impact on how we do things, but it's not even close to being important in the grand scheme of things. I suppose this could be because the Internet does not give you anything new, but rather new ways to do things you've already been doing in the past. Sure it's really convenient, but that is about it.

In addition to it NOT being one of the worlds greatest inventions, the Internet is so poorly designed, that you can catch a computer virus simply by visiting a website, and once this occurs it's possible that everything on your computer is compromised, and worst of all, you may not even know it. I would give the concept of the Internet an "A", but the actual implementation a "D-". I have no idea what the solution is, but I do know that it feels like we've used a lot of duct tape to get where we are now.

Someone or some organization who has a solid understanding of how the current version of the Internet works (both hardware and software), needs to come up with a better solution. Once they have this solution, it should be presented to the public for scrutiny and trial runs to see how it has been improved and what is still vulnerable, and we should not feel rushed into anything for monetary gain, else we risk spending huge resources retooling how the computers connect with one another, only to end up with another shitty duck tape solution.

It is OK to say you don't know something, and that is what I'm doing here. Sure, I've played around a little on the software side of things with HTML, PHP, Java Script, and CSS, but in no way consider myself an expert in any of that, or even close to knowing what specific technical detail is wrong with the Internet. All I know is that I should be able to visit any site on the Internet, click on anything on that web page, attempt to stream any video, receive any email, etc... without the fear of my computer being compromised. Someone, please fix this (without using more duct tape)!

Then again, maybe I'm completely ignorant of the core issues. It **might** be that what I'm asking is impossible, in that maybe all solutions will have an exploitable weakness, and security on the Internet will always suck.

Other Bullshit:

[19] Closed Source Software Used by the Public

Let's pretend you need to buy an automobile. There are 3 main car dealers in town, and you decide to visit each one before making a purchase decision.

You go to store #1 and after looking around a little you see a car that looks nice, but it also looks like someone recently put a fresh coat of paint on it and you are really not sure if this is a good sign or not. When you ask the salesman if you can open the hood, he says NO. You tell the slimy car salesman that you need to look under the hood to make sure the car's engine, transmission, etc... are all in working order. He says it is company policy to never let anyone ever look under the hood, in-fact they have welded the engine compartment shut to prevent this.

After telling the salesman from store #1 to go fuck himself, you travel to store #2. This store has nicer looking cars and also salespeople who are not as creepy. However, when you ask to look under the hood of one of their cars, you get the same response as you got from store #1.

While walking to store #3, you are starting to think there is no hope, and that none of these car dealers will let you examine what's under the hood. When you show up at store #3, you quickly notice that their cars don't look quite as nice as those from the first two stores, and all of their cars have manual transmissions (5-speed stick shift), instead of automatic transmissions, but decide to look at them anyway. You find one you like and ask the salesperson if you can look under the hood and he says, "sure go ahead, you can even take it to a car mechanic who specializes in stuff like that if you want".

After test driving the car from store #3, looking under the hood and having a professional mechanic also verify it has no major defects, you make the decision and buy it.

Of course I'm not really talking about automobiles, I'm talking about computer Operating Systems, specifically those from Microsoft (store #1), Apple (store #2) and others which are based on Linux (store #3).

Computer software can be categorized into 2 types:

1. Open Source
2. Closed Source

Open Source software means people can view the computer code "under the hood" and this makes it much less likely that someone could intentionally place harmful code in it.

Closed Source software means the source code is locked away and nobody can ever look at it. If nobody can inspect the code, it is very easy to hide bugs, back doors, Trojan horses, etc... If someone writes code in such a system to listen, watch or otherwise track what you're doing, you will never know.

Software from Microsoft and Apple are *closed source* (with a few minor exceptions). After reading about how poorly Microsoft is willing to treat the very people who make their software, do you really think they give a shit about their customers (other than their money)?

I have ZERO trust in *closed source* software, and anybody who actually does trust it, is the same kind of idiot who would buy a car whose engine compartment was welded shut.

With all this criticism of *closed source* software, I think there are plenty of things wrong with *open source* software as well, especially their economic model. If you have access to the source code, like in *open source* software, you can easily make a million copies of it, thus trying to sell *open source* software does not really work.

While I'm a firm believer in having the source code publicly available, I'm also a firm believer that the computer programmers who write the code should be compensated for their efforts. All too often, the programmers for *open source* projects just donate their time and are not paid for their efforts.

So, where is the middle ground? On one side you have *closed source* software, which you can sell, but which can also contain "Hitler like" code. On the other side, you have *open source* software, which is much more desirable (for privacy, security, etc...), but which hardly anybody makes money from. The economic model for *open source* computer software just does not fit into any existing models we have used in the past, and we must adapt.

Possible solution #1 Have software companies funded similar to Wikipedia, which runs off of donations. Sure, nobody is going to become a billionaire this way, but at the same time, at least you would have *open source* software and the people who develop it would be compensated for their efforts.

I have no idea how much money the USA spends each year on computer software, but I'm sure it's a lot of money. If the USA, or any of its 50 states, decided that it was going to go completely *open source* for all government computers, public schools, etc..., it could save a ton of money. Instead of spending money on *closed source* software, it could donate a portion of what they were going to spend on *closed source* software to some *open source* software projects they felt were needed.

Possible solution #2 Create a "time-delayed" code repository. When a company wants to release their software, they would add their source code to this special code repository. After a given amount of time (maybe 3 years), the source code is automatically released to the public.

The advantages to this solution are the company has a certain amount of time to make money off of their new software, and the general public would eventually have access to the source code.

For this to work properly, the software would have to be guaranteed somehow to have been compiled using the source code in the time-delayed repository. Without this step, con-artists could release software that was different from the source code.

Making the Switch

If you're using *closed source* software right now and would like to switch to *open source*, some "decent" computer Operating Systems you can try are:

- Debian   // Preferred.
- Ubuntu   // Popular, but I won't use it. If you want to know
              // why, look up their incident with Amazon.com.

Warning: Please consult with a computer professional before making this switch. Switching your computer Operating System will involve things like; backing up your data, deleting everything on your computer, installing a new OS, then restoring your files.

Software you had previously used on Microsoft or Apple computers, is most likely NOT available on a Linux based OS, so you may not be able to use that software anymore, although in some situations there is something similar.

Not all computer hardware is compatible with a Linux based OS.

If you would like to make the switch, but also need access to software programs on Windows or Apple, ask your computer professional about setting up a "dual boot" computer, which would be able to run both Linux and Windows/Apple, but only one of them at a time.

An important distinction should be noted. I'm not saying all computer code should be *open source*, I'm saying all computer code **used by the public** should be *open source*. For example, let's say some company creates some software that it uses ONLY for company purposes and does not involve the public or public data, this software is totally fine to be *closed source* if they want it to be. However, any software that the public uses, or which accesses public data, must be *open source*.

Lastly, if the word "Linux" scares you, and you think that only nerds are capable of using a Linux based OS, just remember that the most popular "smart phone" OS out there right now in 2020 is Android, which is based on Linux. Sure, Linux is different from what you are used to, and will take some time getting used to, but not really any more time than if you had switched between an OS from Microsoft and Apple.

70

Other Bullshit:

[20] Microsoft Forcing Everyone to Have an "NSA account" on *Windows* OS

How many people do you think would use the Microsoft *Windows* Operating System if Microsoft told people that to use the OS, they would first have to create an "NSA account", and login to this account every time they used their computer? Not very many and they would probably go out of business.

Well, of course Microsoft does not force everyone to have an "NSA account", but they have been "forcing" everyone since *Windows 8.1* to have a "Microsoft account".

> Note: I put "forcing" in quotes, since the last OS I used from them (*Windows 8.1*) didn't explicitly offer a "local account" when I installed it, but a search on the Internet revealed a hidden/secret way to get around this, but because this was not a clear option when installing the OS, I'm saying a "Microsoft account" was more or less required.

So what is the difference between an "NSA account" and a "Microsoft account"? Not much. If you had an "NSA account", the NSA (National Security Agency) would have **direct access** to everything on your computer. They would know when you login, what websites you visit, what documents and pictures you have, the people you associate with, basically everything on your computer.

> Note: For citizens of the USA, this "NSA account" would be a direct violation of the 4th Amendment to the Constitution as seen below:
>
> **Amendment IV**
> The right of the people to be secure in their persons, houses, papers, and effects, against unreasonable searches and seizures, shall not be violated, and no Warrants shall issue, but upon probable cause, supported by Oath or affirmation, and particularly describing the place to be searched, and the persons or things to be seized.

The "Microsoft account" is similar to the "NSA account", except the NSA does NOT have direct access to your computer. Actually, I take that back. Since the

Windows OS is *closed source,* and all your data for your "Microsoft account" is stored on Microsoft servers, and the NSA runs programs like PRISM which give it direct access to data from large companies like Microsoft, Google and Apple, via secret courts, we should operate under the assumption that the NSA does indeed have direct access to your "Microsoft account". So there is very little, if any difference between the "Microsoft account" and the theoretical "NSA account" other than one has a slightly nicer name to it.

In a hypothetical world, where humans were not scums sucking maggots and you could actually trust another person/corporation/government to hold onto your data, without them looking at it, this "Microsoft account" idea would be no big deal. However, we don't live in that hypothetical world. We live in a world where if something can be done, it will be done. Even if our own government cleaned up its act, there are many other shitty governments, corporations and/or individuals all around the world willing to do the same thing the NSA and Microsoft are currently doing.

You can't change human nature, so trusting others with your computer data will ALWAYS be a really stupid idea, even with "unbreakable" encryption. So, instead of doing the impossible (changing human nature), do what you can do to create a more secure computing environment, and that is to eliminate "cloud" computing, which the "Microsoft account" basically is.

> Note: Technically, any email provider or "cloud" computing provider which "reads" your email or documents (even via computer program) as it goes across their computer servers is in direct violation of the USA's 4th Amendment which states we have the right to be **"secure in their persons, houses, papers, and effects, against unreasonable searches"**.
>
> Notice how the 4th Amendment does NOT specify WHO can/can't violate your rights, so this applies equally to abuses from government and from corporations. But, as expected, the politicians serve those with money and that is neither you or me but rather large tech companies, so this is another example of corruptocracy in action.

One of the goals of "cloud" computing, besides the easy access to your data for the NSA, is to help you stay organized digitally. When I was a kid in the early 1980's, having a computer in the home was not very common, but over the years eventually most households got one. Later on, instead of having one computer per household, the trend was to have one computer per person. Now in 2020, it is not uncommon for a single person to have multiple computers, like a laptop, desktop, tablet, and/or phone.

A problem arises however when you own more than one computer and you wish to have access the same data from any them. The main issue is that if you create, modify, or delete a file on one computer, it MUST be changed on all the other computers as well, otherwise you end up with two or more computers that have similar, but not exactly the same data on them, which is really bad.

The concept of "cloud" computing is to have a "master copy" of all your files stored someplace, then each of your computers just accesses this "master copy", so if you edit a file on your laptop, the next time you access it on your desktop or phone, you see the updated file. I have no problem with this data synchronization concept. What I have a problem with is WHO holds onto the "master copy" of your files. Microsoft, which has to obey what the NSA tells them to do via secret courts thinks THEY should hold onto your "master copy", and that is bullshit.

If you have more than one computer, there is no technical reason why one of them could not hold onto the "master copy" of your data, as hard disk space is actually quite cheap relatively speaking. Then, the same syncing technology currently used in "cloud" computing could then be converted to sync files only among your computers and NOT with Microsoft or some other company's computer.

Other Bullshit:

[21] Health Care

On January 17th of 2011, I began my 3rd contract at Microsoft. It was the third straight time I was hired to work in the *Windows Phone* department. Once again I found myself working in the same exact Microsoft building, on the same Microsoft product with Microsoft employees... however that's not the issue here. What is at issue, is the way I was treated like a 2nd class employee (because that's really what I was) when it came to work related health issues.

In this contract, Microsoft put me in a room with 3 other contractors. The room was designed to hold 1 or 2 "normal" employees, but since we were 2nd class workers, they just crammed us in there like sardines. They put 4 desks in the room, each pushed up against the 4 walls, in such a way that when we were working, we were facing the walls, and not each other. The room was really too small for this though and while sitting at your desk, if you stretched out your arms, you could reach the person on your left or right. While not ideal, I figured it would be tolerable, that was until I realized that the person to my right was a chain smoker.

The person to my right would go take smoke breaks a number of times each day. When he would come back, since we were crammed in the room so tight, the stench of smoke that would follow him would just about knock me over it was so bad. I had picked up running about 5 years earlier, so not only did it stink, but I didn't appreciate having to breath this guys nasty habit for 8 hours a day. But wait, it gets worse! After he would come back from his smoke break outside, he would start smoking an e-cigarette inside right next to me.

It was not long after I starting working there that I noticed a burning sensation when I breathed, even after work when I was at home. As someone who liked to run, and who also had an uncle and grandfather who both died of lung cancer, this really made me mad that I was being exposed to this bullshit.

So, I inquired to my supervisor (a "real" Microsoft employee) about getting assigned to an office with non-smokers, or to have the smoker moved to an office with other smokers. The result was Fuck You, you're just a 2nd class worker, you have no rights. That was the message, but of course it was stated in a more politically correct way.

> Note: I liked working for that supervisor and I believe he genuinely tried to find me a different office, but it was either someone above him, or "the system" which prevented this office change.

I also brought it up with my contracting company, *Volt Technical Services*, but as expected they could not, or would not, do anything, as their only real job was to take a cut of each of my paychecks and NOT to stand up for me or my working conditions.

This whole situation was very frustrating for me. Then one evening after work, having that burning feeling still in my lungs, I decided to take a drive up to the mountains to get some fresh air and left the sunroof of my car open to let in as much clean air as possible to try to clean out my lungs. While I was on my drive, I noticed a billboard advertising a medical facility at the next exit. Then I got a great idea. I just need to get my body tested to see if I have something like nicotine or some other smoking bi-product in my body. Then, I'd be able to go back to Microsoft and *Volt Technical Services* and have something firm to stand on when I made my request to be moved away from this 2nd hand smoke and e-cigarette bullshit.

I was healthy enough to walk in the door myself and calmly tell them what I was there for. Then, they took me to a room where tests were to be performed. Apparently, all they saw was a middle aged man who was having breathing issues. They didn't really focus on what I very specifically asked for. Not being a doctor, nurse or having any real medical background, I figured the tests they were doing were to help me prove my body was infected with smoking products as I had requested.

One of the first things they wanted to do was take a blood sample, and this made total sense to me. I was thinking they would use this blood sample to do some chemical analysis on it to see what was in my blood stream. However, their incompetence was incredible. The first person failed to find the vein in my arm after a few tries. Then, she brought in another person, who also tried and failed. Then, they brought in a 3rd person, who decided it was "too complicated" to take a blood sample the normal way, and instead of using a simple needle, they had some elaborate contraption, which I'm sure cost more money and presto they finally were able to take a blood sample from my arm. Like I said before, I have no medical training, but I do have a niece who is a nurse, and vividly remember her going wild about how great the veins in my arm were and how easy it would be to access them via needle.

After the blood sample was finally taken, they proceeded to run many other types of tests, but at the end of the hospital visit, they said something to the effect of "well, you're not having a heart attack, but were not sure what is wrong with you". I then asked, if they were able to tell if there was nicotine or some other smoking or e-cigarette product in my blood stream, and he said, "oh, we can't do those kind of tests here". What the Fuck! I had explicitly stated when I showed up, that is what I wanted done. They just ignored all that, and ran a bunch of unnecessary tests. If they would have told me upfront that they couldn't do those kind of tests at that facility, I would have walked out the door and continued on my road trip up to the mountains and/or maybe setup an appointment with another place which could run those type of tests.

So after being there for about 1.5 hours, and not accomplishing anything, I walked out and wondered how expensive it would be. I had health insurance at the time, so I figured it would not be too bad of a financial hit... boy was I ever wrong about that.

You would think that health care would be the same as any other product or service where you're told what you'll get and also how much it will cost, BEFORE you agree to buy it. Well, apparently the health care system in *The United States of America* works a little differently, and NOT in a good way.

Have you ever seen the classic movie "Vacation" staring Chevy Chase? **Movie "Spoiler Alert" in affect for rest of this paragraph!** Well, on his family's road trip across the country, they have some car problems. They have it repaired at the only place available and when it comes time to pay for it, Chevy Chase's character asks "What do I owe you?", and the unscrupulous mechanic replies with "How much you got?". That is the perfect analogy for how the health care and health insurance systems in *The United States of America* work.

Turns out the final bill was almost six-thousand dollars! That is the price of a decent used car. There is no way in hell I would have ever agreed to that upfront. While my insurance did cover most of it, I still had to fork out about one-thousand dollars out of my own pocket! What's even worse than this outrageous bill, is my understanding that the bill total was complicated for the medical facility to figure out, since they are able to charge different rates, depending on what kind of insurance I had, and thus you now understand the movie analogy.

I seriously tried the calm collective logical approach the first few times I made the request to change offices, but when that didn't work, and I kept hearing there was nothing that could be done, I had to lower myself to basically whining and bitching like a little brat until Microsoft caved in and finally agreed to move me to a different location in the same building. It really sucked to know that I felt like I was the bad guy for making such demands, but there was no way in hell I was going to be subjected to 2nd hand smoke and direct exposure to e-cigarettes for 8 hours a day. Once again, Fuck You Microsoft.

The new location they put me in was a large open room NOT designed for humans, but rather it was designed for computer servers. The humming sound of computers running was very noticeable, and it was colder than most rooms, so I often wore a coat, but it was much better than sitting arms length away from a chain smoker. At the time, there was only a handful of other 2nd class workers in that large room, but over the course of that year and my next contract in which I worked the same exact job and was working in that same room, Microsoft decided this hole in the ground was a great place to stick 2nd class employees and thus filled the room up as much as they possibly could with disposable 2nd class workers, but not a single "regular" Microsoft employee ever got stuck in such a shit hole.

Wouldn't you know it, a little while after I changed offices, this burning lung issue went away. Coincidence? I think not!

So, that concludes my bullshit medical experience at Microsoft, but I'm left with lots of questions.

- Why are cigarettes still manufactured and sold, when they've been proven to cause cancer? We had no problem banning Asbestos products, so why not cigarettes?
- Given the history of cigarettes and the countless people they have killed, why are e-cigarettes not put under a HUGE microscope and heavily scrutinized (and possibly banned) for any ill health effects (if found)?
- Microsoft would never have any of its employees (even the 2nd class type) work right next to a literal pile of stinky bullshit, so why was it so hard to get them do the simple thing and separate me from this stinky smoker, even though I counted at least a half dozen completely empty offices on the same floor of the building I was at, and even brought this up in my move request.
- Why does a 1.5 hour medical visit cost almost six-thousand dollars?
- Why don't medical facilities let you know the exact price of everything they offer **before it's done**, especially if you're in a non-life-threating situation?
- Why can medical facilities charge different rates depending on the type of insurance you have?
- How long before "Health Care" and "Health Insurance" become a synonym for "Evil" in the USA (if it hasn't already)?

You could try to analyze each and every one of these questions separately, but at their core, if you boil it down to one issue which led to all this bullshit, it is **corruptocracy**. A government, which represents the rich and powerful, and NOT the average citizens is easily manipulated into creating bullshit conditions like these. You could try to take on and fix each of these issues separately, but until you eradicate corruptocracy, any minor success you may have will be overshadowed by ten new piles of bullshit.

Other Bullshit:

[22] The Big Lie Students are Taught About Electricity

> **Warning:** Do not attempt to replicate this electrical circuit unless you are properly trained. Improper setup could result in electric shock, or an electrical short, which would cause the battery to overheat and possibly catch fire. Also, the circuit is just a general diagram, and is missing key info like battery voltage, required wire thickness, an on/off switch, a safety fuse to protect against shorts, the possible need for a resistor, etc...

Take a look at the simple diagram below. There is a battery, a light bulb, and wire connecting the two. Assuming the battery is charged up, electricity will flow through this circuit and the light bulb will turn on. Now answer this question: **What direction do you think the electricity will flow?**

1. From the "+" battery terminal, through the light bulb, then to the "-" battery terminal?

2. From the "-" battery terminal, through the light bulb, then to the "+" battery terminal?

If you were "educated" in the United States, there is a good chance you got the wrong answer. In this circuit, the only thing that flows are electrons, and electrons are negatively charged. If we take a closer look at the circuit with a "special" magnifying glass, we can look at one of these electrons in the circuit.

Now think back to what you know about magnets. Remember that "opposite charges" attract one another, and "similar charges" repel each other. Since electrons are negatively charged, they are attracted to the "+" battery terminal and trying to get away from the "-" terminal.

So, the answer is, the electricity flows from the negative "-" terminal of the battery, through the wire, through the light bulb and then ends up at the positive "+" terminal of the battery.

Tradition sucks when it prevents progress. Apparently the reason why many schools (even universities) still teach their students that electricity flows in a metal circuit from "+" to "-", is because that was the way it was first understood and taught, and apparently it does not matter when trying to understand a circuit, thus they keep teaching the wrong way, since that is the way it has always been done. That way of thinking is wrong, it creates confusion, and of course it's bullshit.

> Note: I do **NOT** have a degree in Electrical Engineering, but have tried to teach myself through reading books and playing with simple circuits, so the info I presented here may be inaccurate, but it is my current understanding of the subject and believe it to be correct.

Other Bullshit:

[23] College

Learning is important, but college is full of bullshit.

Why do we have colleges, or any schools for that matter?

- Do they exist to generate income like a business?
- Do they exist so the NFL can have a semi-pro football league to recruit from?
- Do they exist to help subsidize the text book industry?
- Do they exist so rich bankers can live off of the interest payments made by young people just starting out in life?

In *The United States of America*, the answer to all those questions is unfortunately YES, and that is bullshit.

Why do I think we have colleges and other schools? A robot can be assembled, turned on for the first time and have all the knowledge previously gained by its predecessors, pre-programmed into it. Humans are different. You can take a male and female human, both with multiple college degrees in science, art and history, but when those two humans mate and create a baby, that baby does not inherit any of that knowledge. This is why we have schools: To teach all the new humans coming into the world what the previous humans were already able to learn, and also provide them with critical thinking and problem solving skills so they can find solutions to problems their parents were not yet able to solve.

In short, every human born in today's "advanced" society starts off with the same knowledge as babies born 100 or 1000 years ago. If you don't educate them, or miss-educate them with propaganda, they are literally no better off than people who lived in the dark ages.

Solution

Rethink our entire approach to the higher education process. Instead of thinking that it is the student who should pay for the education, change that around and realize it is society which owes them the opportunity to learn what we already know. I guess this is sort of like "pay it forward". When you enter this world, you would be given a free education, but it is also your responsibility later on, as a tax payer, to foot the bill for the next generation to learn what we've learned.

I would make these changes, to help realize that goal:

- All of this will be done on the taxpayer's dime, so in a way everyone pays for college, but also, everyone can go to college as well.
- Create a new college, or convert an existing one as a trial for these ideas, so any issues seen can be ironed out before we expand to other colleges.
- All housing is free for students. All meals are free for students. The students would basically not have to pay a single dime to stay there and learn. They are welcome to stay as long as they maintain acceptable grades.
- As much as possible, all text books will be written for "e-ink" type electronic books, like the Amazon Kindle, but NOT like the iPad, or Surface tablets as those don't have the nice paper-like viewing surface. However, we won't be using the Amazon Kindle, since Amazon tracks what books each Kindle has on it, and can even "burn" the book (AKA delete it) at their own discretion. This electronic book burning and/or tracking is bullshit.
- The government will pay people to create the electronic-text-books, but the book writer is paid a one time fee for their services, not for each copy of the electronic text book. Maybe reserve the option to give a bonus to writers whose books become popular and/or well reviewed.
- There will be zero football, tennis, basketball, golf, or other semi-pro teams. However, there will be a fitness center where the students can get exercise and possibly even play some of those sports with their friends. Exercise is very important for everyone, not just professional athletes.
- The campus would be entirely owned by the state or federal government, and not in rented out buildings where year after year money is wasted on rent.
- It would be a combination of what we now consider "college + trade school". That is, you could learn calculus and also how to weld steel at the same campus.

- Lastly, re-evaluate the entire learning process.
    - From my experience, school was like a treadmill set at a fixed speed. Some people were fine learning at that speed, others got overwhelmed (like myself), and yet others were bored. There needs to be more opportunity for students to learn at a pace suited for them.
    - Currently, schools like to teach once, test once, then move on to another subject. Maybe this works for a few people, but I think that the majority of the population needs a little more repetition for material to really sink in. When you "learn" something, you should be able to pass a test for it now, plus in one week, one month and one year from now. Otherwise, you didn't really learn it!

Since learning takes effort, and some people would rather stay home and play a video game or watch TV, I think there should be some sort of additional tax placed upon people who don't achieve a certain level of education. We could call this the "stupid tax", and sooner or later the lazy bums will get tired of paying this tax and go get educated, which is what society expects of them.

What do we, as a society get out of this?

- Businesses would have access to a pool of workers that are far more educated and/or skilled than they are now.
- Frees young people just starting out in life, to be free from financial debt, but at the same time, have the education and skills needed to become productive citizens.

Extreme Warning: Colleges need to once again become a place where "diversity of ideas" are allowed to be spoken. Not that all ideas are good, but we should be open to at least listening to a variety of ideas, then having discussions on the merits of them.

Note: Taxpayers in the USA already pay for public education for K-12, so what's the big deal for a few more years, especially if we learn to reduce the costs of education.

Other Bullshit:

[24] Multiple Human Languages

A long time ago, when the human population on the planet was low, different groups of people were separated by large swaths of land and water, and not having any technology to connect one group of people with another, each group developed their own language. However, now that the population of the human race has grown so large that you can hardly go anywhere without bumping into another human, and our technology enables us to communicate via speech or written word instantly anywhere in the world, the continued use of all these languages is bullshit.

For some reason, humans think that it's noble to use the languages of the past, and people who know more than one are considered sophisticated. All someone has to do is look at the news, and by activating a few brain cells realize that lack of a common language helps enable one group of people to dehumanize another group, and once that is done, convincing the masses to wage war against the "dumb fucks" from the other group is much easier. To put it another way, if all you hear is "moo", or "blah, blah, blah", the chances of you caring about this other creature are much less than if it says something you can understand, like "Hello, my name is Fred."

Creating a single common language among the entire human population will not eliminate all wars, but it will dramatically reduce conflict between groups of people and when war does occur, at least you will know exactly what the other people are saying, and have the ability to evaluate the positions each side has taken and why you're fighting, without depending on questionable translations.

I'm not saying everyone should speak English, French, Russian, Chinese, or some other language. I'm saying we need to find one language and agree to teach it to the next generation of humans. Maybe this common language already exists, or maybe it doesn't and people who are skilled with languages and figuring out what makes a language easy to understand and also flexible, so new words can be added, could create it. Simply picking the language which is most prevalent is not necessarily the right thing to do. Pick or create the right language, regardless of its current popularity, as this is a monumental undertaking that will literally take generations to implement.

I'm sure someone will make the argument that some sort of instant translator technology will eliminate the need for this single human language, but I'd disagree with that because as it has multiple issues:

- Not everyone will be able to afford it.
- If the translation is wrong, or even slightly inaccurate, it could lead to conflict.
- Who wants to carry around tech all the time, and even if it's very small, do we really want implants in our body?
- What if something like a computer virus, electromagnetic pulse, or something else disables the technology? The entire world would be back to square one again.

If you're looking for an example of how multiple languages can make basic communication difficult, I'd recommend watching; Star Trek: The Next Generation: Season 5, Episode 2 "Darmok".

Other Bullshit:

[25] Human Behavior

United Parcel Service (UPS) is in the business of moving boxes all around the world. Before you can move a box, you have to pick it up. Since moving boxes around is their specialty, they have come up with the "8 keys to lifting and lowering". These eight keys to lifting and lowering give their employees very specific techniques they can use to properly lift a box, move it, then lower it.

What these 8-keys to lifting and lower are doesn't matter for this chapter. What matters is that UPS noticed their employees were getting injured lifting boxes, so they came up with a short list of very specific techniques their employees could use so they could lift a box without hurting their back or other part of their body.

This is the same kind of systematic analysis and problem solving which needs to be applied to human behavior. For example, when someone experiences a strong emotion like hate, jealousy, rejection, or love, how do we teach humans to deal with these? Do we have "The 8 keys to dealing with anger"? No we don't, but we should.

I mentioned earlier on in the book that each new human born into this world starts off with a blank slate and needs to be educated, otherwise they are no better off than early cave dwelling humans. Part of this education MUST include ways for these new humans to learn how to deal with these strong emotions.

These techniques for dealing with stuff like frustration, love, jealousy, etc... need to be simple enough to memorize, and they must be taught from an early age, then reviewed over and over again. So, for example, Alice would be taught in 1st grade how to handle the situation where she gets mad at someone. In the 2nd grade, her teachers would review these techniques and make sure she remembered them, and this process would be repeated all the way up until she graduated from college. These skills need to be second nature, so when humans do experience one of these emotions, they know how to properly deal with it, instead of the instincts we are all born with, some of which are not very pretty.

So what are these specific techniques? I have no idea. I just know that reading the news everyday is a constant reminder of how desperately they are needed. Someone out there who is knowledgeable in human behavior needs to design these techniques, get schools to teach them, then refine as needed.

Just hoping that humans will naturally know how to properly handle these situations, then locking them up in a cage when they get it wrong is not the correct approach, at least for an intelligent species.

Other Bullshit:

[26] Human Population

> Note: This chapter is exactly the same as the 2015 version of this book, and before I had ever heard of Thanos and "the snap".

Two things that the Mormon church strongly encourage and/or requires of its members are:

1. Church members are to pay 10% of their income to the church.
2. Church members are encouraged to have as many babies as possible.

Do you think that just maybe, these two things are possibly connected in some way? For example, if there are more church members, that means there are more people giving you 10% of their income. The Mormon church is by no means the only religion which pushes people to have large families, I just single them out since that's the church I was raised in.

Have you ever been in stop-and-go traffic on your way to/from work and thought to yourself, "Hey, the world would be such a better place if there were just more people in it"? Yeah, I didn't think so.

Now is the about the time when someone reading this book will say the problem is the automobile and we just need to be using more public transportation. I'm not saying public transportation is a bad thing at all, but in parts of the world like India where they have over a billion people, I've seen pictures of Indians riding their public train system and the trains are so full, that people are actually sitting on top of the train while it moves, so public transportation alone will not fix the over-crowding issue.

According to various sources on the Internet (like Wikipedia), there are a little over 7 billion humans on planet Earth (as of 2014). Would the world be twice as great if it had 14 billion people? If not, why?

I would make the argument that the world would be better off with a lower human population. For example, if there were only 3.5 billion people (½ of the current population), that would mean there would be twice as much land per person, half as many cars on the road, etc...

Some people will make the argument that humans should be able to have as many kids as they want, and thus who cares about the total world population, we'll just let it grow until it reaches its maximum carrying capacity. You want to know what other creature reproduces like that? Tribbles, from the Star Trek. Sure, you can argue that they are fictional creatures, but I figured you'd appreciate that comparison a little more than if I had compared humans to a virus.

I've thrown some number out there, like 3.5 billion, 7 billion, 14 billion. None of them really matter though. What matters is that "if" humans are truly intelligent, and that is a big fucking "IF", they will be able to decide on what the ideal human population should be, then do their best to maintain that number, avoiding fluctuations up or down to the best of their ability.

Right now, the United States has a tax system that benefits those who have more kids. This is a direct way of encouraging the population to have more babies. I challenge the United States to decide on what its population goal should be, and have strict guidelines for maintaining it. If that means each female can have a maximum of 1 or 2 kids before her tubes are tied, so be it. Sticking to the population goal also means being very strict on how many people we let into the country via immigration.

What makes the human species great has absolutely nothing to do with the quantity of humans on the planet, but rather the quality of the humans that are on it. Also, the quality of a human has nothing to do with the color of their skin, the language they speak, how old they are, if they have a penis or vagina, or any thing else like that.

EVERY human born into this world is capable of being a quality person, but all to often "the system" lets them down. For example:

- They are not educated.
- They are mis-educated via propaganda and not taught how to think for themselves.
- Their parent(s), who should be teaching them about life and proper human behavior are too busy working to provide food and shelter for them that they are left to learn this stuff on their own.
- Their parent(s) and/or sibling(s) are emotionally and/or physically abusive to them and they spend their whole childhood in basic survival mode. By the time they reach adulthood, they become parents themselves and the cycle often repeats itself.

If you really want to make this world a better place, you need to understand a few things.

- As long as humans have to fight and claw for the basics of life, like food and shelter, you will continue to have war and violence.

- An economic system that will collapse if people stop buying stuff they don't need is bullshit.

- Unlike an automobile or a phone, land is free. That is, humans had absolutely nothing to do with how the land got there.

- Each human born into this world should be assigned the right to occupy their own little part of this planet. At the same time, they should not be allowed to occupy more than their allotted amount of land.

- Since a human didn't create the land, they technically have no right to sell it to someone else. A human could however give up their claim to a specific plot of land and then claim another unoccupied plot of land somewhere else.

If the human species is actually intelligent, it would:

- Set a goal for what its total population should be and maintain it to the best of their ability.

- Properly educate its newest members.

- Provide a plot of land for each member, so they don't have to fight over it.

- Create one common language, so they can all communicate with each other.

There are some intelligent humans, but collectively the entire species is not very bright at all. They continue to wage war with one another and fight for basic resources and are completely delusional if they think things will get any better if they just hope or pray for peace, or think that technology will solve this.

I will make this guarantee to you right now. If the human species does not do some serious introspection and try to figure out the root cause of all this violence and war, eventually their technology and hubris will get out of control and they will wipe themselves out. Maybe not today, or tomorrow, but it will happen.

Other Bullshit:

[27] Microsoft's Contracting Companies

If you've been reading this book from front to back, you've already heard some of my rants about the evils of Microsoft, both as an employer and the actual software they make. Here's a summary so far:

- As a contractor, I would work in a Microsoft building, on Microsoft software, and with Microsoft's "normal" employees, but was NOT a Microsoft employee, but rather a 2nd class worker.
- There are 2 types of Microsoft contractors. "a-" and "v-".
    - "a-" contractors can only work for 12 months, then Microsoft mandates that they take 100 days off, during which time they are eligible for unemployment benefits.
    - "v-" contractors can in theory work forever as a 2nd class worker, with no mandatory break.
- From my six years of personal experience as a Microsoft contractor working in both the *Windows Phone* and *XBox* departments, I would guesstimate that approximately ¼th of all the tech people working in those departments were contractors, but Microsoft never releases information on this.
- When Microsoft has massive layoffs like they did in 2009 and 2014, they are not required by law, nor do they voluntarily mention how many contractors are let go and/or not re-hired after their mandatory break. The number of people they mention laid off are ONLY Microsoft employees. It's as if contractors don't exist, and are truly 2nd class workers.
- Software from Microsoft is almost completely closed source, so if they want to add code which will secretly tap into your microphone, camera, GPS, or otherwise track what you do and where you go, what you read, who you communicate with, there really is nothing you can do to stop them or even know if this is being done at all.
- Starting with *Windows 8.1*, Microsoft has **strongly** encouraged and/or made it next to impossible to create a user account on their *Windows* Operating System without having a "Microsoft / NSA account".
- Microsoft has used "secure boot" as a way to make it impossible to install any other Operating System on the *Surface RT* tablet, and this

"secure boot" seems to be required on all computers sold with their OS, so it's possible that in the future they could lock down all *Windows* computers and prevent other Operating Systems from being used (like Linux).

- The two contracting companies I "worked for" while at Microsoft; *Volt Technical Services* -and- *Insight Global*, both placed questionably legal requirements in my employee contract that said I could not switch to a different contracting company for 30-80 days past the 100 day mandatory break Microsoft made me take.

- *Insight Global* put a clause in my contract that said I could not speak my mind about how I liked or disliked working for them, thus forcing 2nd class workers to keep their mouths shut.

- In the hiring process, the only thing the contracting companies do is act like a middle man and pass my resume to Microsoft. The job interviews were performed in Microsoft buildings, by Microsoft employees.

- Microsoft uses contractors NOT for some one-time project like Y2K, but for most, if not all, of their ongoing long-term software projects.

- Since contractors are not Microsoft employees, they don't receive benefits a "normal" Microsoft employee would receive, even though both the "normal" employee and the contractor work side by side on the same software in the same building.

- Even though Microsoft contractors get paid by the hour and are not working for a fixed salary, if a contractor works more than 40 hours in a week, they don't get overtime pay (1.5 times normal wage), but rather get paid at their regular rate.

- The contracting companies produce nothing and contribute absolutely nothing to society. They make their living by taking a cut of each paycheck from all of their "employees", thus they are literal parasites.

- Microsoft will at times place their 2nd class workers in a shitty physical environment which they would NEVER place one of their "normal" employees in.

- Microsoft created a huge placard with the names of "all" the people who worked on the *XBox One*, but didn't include any of the names of the contractors who also worked on it, thus proving there is an upper and lower class of people at Microsoft.

- Microsoft hired me 5 separate times over six years to work as a contractor, but not once did they ever offer to hire me as a "normal" employee, but still complain to politicians (AKA bribe them with campaign contributions) that they "can't find enough qualified workers" here in the USA. The politicians then grant them permission to bring in more H1-B visa workers from around the world.

With all that said, what could I possibly have left to criticize of Microsoft? It has to do with the parasitic contracting companies Microsoft uses for it's 2nd class workforce, and how MUCH money these companies suck out of their workers paychecks.

> **Note:** I would normally not talk about specific wages, nor is this meant to be seen as bragging of any kind. Maybe you're working for minimum wage and have a hard time relating to the troubles of someone making so much more than you. The point I'm trying to make here affects all wage groups, not just the ones making "decent" wages, so even if you're at the bottom making minimum wage, this affects you too (if you're a contractor and not a regular employee where you work).

Here is a breakdown of the wages I received during my 5 contracts at Microsoft. My job title was "Software Development Engineer in Test".

1. Started at $25.50, but when Wall Street crashed in 2008, Microsoft forced a 10% wage reduction to $22.95, even though some said it was illegal for Microsoft to change the agreed upon wage in the contract.
2. $28.16 / hour
3. $32.58 / hour
4. $43.00 / hour
5. $48.75 / hour

My first 3 contracts I worked for *Volt Technical Services*. Wait, I take that back, I didn't really work FOR them, as they don't actually build or produce anything, and I didn't work in their buildings, but they were classified as my employer and took a cut of each and every paycheck I received.

As mentioned above, my first contract wage started out at $25.50 / hour. I was fresh out of college, desperate for work, and not familiar with how expensive it was to live in Redmond Washington. When I was searching for work, *Volt* asked me how much I was willing to work for. I just told them $25 / hour, since I had no idea what I should really ask for. Turns out, that was a really low wage for the position I was hired for, but *Volt* didn't tell me that.

Fast forward a few years and let me tell you what happened while I was looking to get hired for my 4th contract position. Like I mentioned before, I had worked my first 3 contracts with *Volt Technical Services*, but had started off at a real low wage (relatively speaking), and I was starting to feel like I was paying for this on each new contract, since *Volt* didn't want to boost me up to where I "should" be, but rather just incremental pay increases according to where I started out at.

When I worked the previous contract, I did an excellent job and my supervisor was real pleased with my work, but I was an "a-" contractor so I had to take the mandatory 100 day break and that is what I did. When the time came for me to look for contract #4, *Volt* told me that Microsoft wanted me back real bad for that same position, and I would not even have to interview for the job (which was unusual). All I would have to do was sign some papers and I could start work as soon as my mandatory 100 day break ran out.

This time however, Microsoft wanted me to come back as a "v-" contractor, so I wouldn't have to take the mandatory 100 day break anymore. I thought that was great, and I asked *Volt* what my pay would be for contract #4 and they said $31.00 / hour, which was $1.58 / hour LESS than my previous contract!

What the fuck? I did an excellent job in contract #3, and Microsoft wanted me back so bad for the same exact position, that they are not even going to require me to interview for it, and *Volt* had the balls to tell me that I would be making less money. Their explanation was that since I worked the last contract as an "a-", and I would now be a "v-" contractor, there was less money in it. I said bullshit!

I wrote *Volt Technical Services* a long letter explaining my grievances and how I felt I was being exploited and basically demanded one of these two options:

1. $40 / hour for this new contract.
2. Release me from my questionably legal waiting period so I could work with a different parasite for my next contract at Microsoft.

Volt said the money just was not there, and they released me. Turns out *Volt* was full of shit. I was able to get another parasite to pay me $43 / hour for that very same job. That is a difference of $24,960 per year that one parasite was wanting to suck from me MORE than the other parasite.

I have no idea what the total amount the parasite was sucking from me, but the fact that the difference between the two parasites was almost twenty-five thousand dollars, was just enough to make the blood boil.

So, in this contract I was making $43 / hour instead of $31 / hour, and most of you probably don't care, as you're thinking even the lower wage would be awesome. That is not the point. The point is, this parasite (*Volt Technical Services*) was willing to siphon off AT LEAST 28% of my income. If you're working for a contracting company (doing any kind of work) and making $10 / hour, but your contracting company is siphoning off 28% of your income, this really means you should be receiving $13.89 / hour.

Now, ponder these questions:

- Do you really think that politicians are looking out for the American worker, or are they looking out for the ultra rich people and organizations like Microsoft who put them in office with big bribes (AKA campaign contributions)?
- Do you really still think that bribes (AKA campaign contributions) in the election process are good for Americans?
- Are you ready to demand the political election changes described in the first chapter?
- Are you ready for the *Turing Employment Center*, which would eliminate a lot of other bad stuff like racism, ageism and sexism from the employment hiring process?

If you think that what we need are more unions to fix many of these workplace conditions, I would disagree with that. In the United States, I can't think of a city where unions have had more control/influence than Detroit Michigan with the auto industry. What kind of city is Detroit today? It's a shit hole. What we need are politicians that actually represent the people, rather than just representing those who are able to bribe them with campaign contributions.

Other Bullshit:

[28] Mormon Church's View of Masturbation

How would you feel if every time you ate something (even healthy foods), you were told you were fat, unwanted and that you just needed to have more self control and stop doing that? Hopefully, you recognize that is bullshit. What if we take it one step further, and it is your church leaders doing the shaming?

I was born and raised Mormon and went through a similar shaming process, but instead of being told I was "bad" for eating, I was told I was "bad" for releasing my sexual desires via masturbating.

When I was growing up, the "official doctrine" of the Mormon church regarding masturbation came from a pamphlet called **"To Young Men Only"**. The Mormon church may say this is not "official doctrine", but fuck them. Any material you promote for 38+ years IS the official policy of the church.

In reference to masturbation, here's a few select quotes from the pamphlet.

- "He has decreed serious penalties indeed for the misuse of it."
- "You are forbidden to use them now in order that you may use them with worthiness and virtue and fullness of joy at the proper time in life."
- "For the most part, unless you tamper with it, you will hardly be aware that it is working at all."
- "You may already have been guilty of tampering with these powers. You may even have developed a habit. What do you do then?"

Obviously, the advice I got when I was young was quite horrible. Instead of the advice I got, I wish I had read a pamphlet which looked more like the info below...

> **Start of my theoretical pamphlet (NOT the Mormon version).**

In reference to being shamed for eating... If you're shamed after eating often enough, you might even start to believe that what you are doing is wrong. Even when nobody was around to say the shameful words, you would feel it inside and this can lead to low self esteem, eating disorders and depression.

Eating is a natural function of the human body. When we are born, we don't have any teeth and start off with milk, then soft foods like applesauce, then eventually we grow teeth and can grind up our own food.

Besides eating, there are other natural human bodily functions, like urinating when your bladder gets full, defecating when your body needs to get rid of unabsorbed foods you had previously eaten, and also sex.

Just like hunger pains tell us our bodies needs food or we will we eventually starve to death, sexual desires remind us that we need to mate or our species will go extinct. Both hunger and sex are very strong internal desires and you should not feel shameful for having them as they are a normal part of being human.

Sometimes these sexual desires arouse inside of you, but you don't have a partner to engage in sex with. What do you do then? The solution to this is **masturbation**. Masturbation for both males and females is normal. When you learn how your body works and how to reach orgasm, you will find this as a way to ease those sexual desires, relax and reduce stress.

Not only should you learn how to pleasure your own body, you should also learn how the opposite sex pleasures themselves. When you know how to pleasure your sexual partner, you will find it can help strengthen the bond between the two of you.

Just like some humans eat more food than others, the same can be said for sexual desire. Sex drive can vary from human to human, and nobody should be shamed for having too little or too high of a sex drive. When two sexual partners have different sex drives, it can be frustrating for one or both of them and masturbation can help relieve the sexual desires of the hornier person, or when their partner is not around, or not in the mood for sex.

The human species has various written and unwritten rules they abide by. For example, wearing a bathing suit, or no clothes at all, may be accepted as normal at the beach, but not in a fancy restaurant. These rules change over time and vary from one location to another. The same goes for acts of sexuality. Feel free to have sexual experiences in places other than your bedroom with the lights off and under the covers. However, also be aware of local laws and customs, so not to offend others.

Whatever the written and unwritten rules your community abides by, there should NEVER be a law anywhere which turns any consenting sexual behavior into such a crime that the punishment is greater than that for any other bodily function. For example, it seems reasonable that a law is in place that says not to urinate or defecate on a public sidewalk. If some person(s) were to engage in a sexual act in that same place, the punishment should be no greater than if the person(s) had urinated or defecated in that same location. Urinating, defecating and sex are all normal bodily functions, and while it is fine to make laws saying there are places not to do these things, the punishment for sexual based bodily functions should never differ from that of other bodily functions.

Unwelcome physical contact is a violation of someones body, and is not always sexual, but it can be. This unwelcome physical contact can vary from simply placing a hand on someones shoulder, a kiss, feeling the buttocks or chest, touching the genitalia, and sexual intercourse. As a responsible human, you need to learn when you can and can't physically touch another person.

Not all human communication is verbal. If you greet someone and they extend their hand towards you, they most likely want to shake your hand, and this is a normal greeting in some cultures. The person didn't have to say "May I shake your hand?", it was implied. You are free to shake or not shake.

If you have NOT had sexual contact with a specific person before, it is wrong to just reach out and start touching them without their express permission. How do you go about getting this permission? Well, you could just ask "Can I touch your butt?", or something like that, but I would venture to guess that many people will be put off by this request. It's best to start at the beginning and go from there. For example, a good place to start is, "May I hold your hand?". If the person turns down your request to hold hands, you can be pretty certain that they would also turn down a request to kiss them or engage in sexual intercourse.

If you ask to hold hands, and the person agrees, this ONLY meant they agreed to hold hands. It didn't mean they gave you permission to touch other parts of their body other than their hand. Like I mentioned before though, some human communication is non-verbal. You might pick up a sign by the way the person is caressing your hand that they want to increase the amount of physical contact. While, it may be implied that they are ready to kiss you, it does not guarantee that. If you misread their non-verbal communication for the kiss, and you attempt to kiss anyway, and they back away or say something to indicate they don't want to kiss you, stop the attempt to kiss them and don't assume any other non-verbal communication with them.

Use the **3 Stages of Permission** listed below when you want to make physical contact with someone for the first time.

1. Hold their hand.
2. Kiss and touch.
3. Sexual intercourse.

One of the great things about the "3 stages", is that everyone used them, this would reduce confusion and conflict when humans are trying to mate with each other. The first stage of "hold their hand" is VERY important. The reason for this, is because it's a very minor thing to request and/or deny.

Some people may give you permission to progress through the 3 stages quicker than others. Some may let you get to stage 1 or 2, but never to stage 3. Individuals also have the right to revoke any of the permissions previously granted to someone else. This is in their right, as it is their body you are wishing to make contact with.

Sexual fantasies are similar to food cravings. You may think that chocolate cake is the greatest food in the whole world, but you would not eat it for every meal. If you're in a committed relationship with someone and find yourself having sexual fantasies about someone else, does this mean you no longer love the person you're in a relationship with? Of course not.

The reason why you will sometimes have sexual desires for people other than the person you are committed to, is the human species thrives on mixing the gene pool. It's normal to have these feelings, but it does not necessarily mean you need to act on them. Maybe your partner wants to hear about your fantasies, and maybe they don't, and maybe their fantasy is that you only fantasize about them and nobody else. Maybe your partner will want to role play with you and pretend to be the other person, or maybe they will want to help you act out this fantasy in real life. Be open and honest with your sexual partner.

Some religious organizations perform **circumcision** on their new born babies or young adults. This is when "extra" skin is removed from the genitalia. These acts are barbaric, a violation against the body and there should be sever consequences for the parents who allow this to be done as well as for the person who performs the circumcision.

In conclusion, sex can be very fun and exciting, but if you want to engage in it, you must understand the possible consequences.

- Sex is how babies are created, and raising a baby to be a well adjusted adult is a huge responsibility. If the sperm from the male reaches the egg in the woman, a pregnancy can begin. There are ways to reduce this risk, like using a condom, or some other forms of birth control.

- Some diseases are spread with sexual contact. It is important to know which ones are curable and which are not. Also, learn how you and your sexual partner(s) can get tested for these, and how to properly use a condom, which can reduce chances of spreading disease.

- Masturbation is the safest sex of all, as it won't spread disease or result in an unwanted pregnancy.

> **End of my theoretical pamphlet (NOT the Mormon version).**

Mormons don't have the attitude that they "think" their god might exist, they "know" their god exists. There is no room for doubt and especially not any room for people openly questioning anything. If the church leaders say something, this is the same as it coming directly from god, since after all, the Mormon Prophet and his 12 Apostles supposedly have direct contact with god via "**prophecy, revelation, visions**" as spelled out in their "Articles of Faith".

Mormon "Articles of Faith" 7 and 12. (See Appendix A, for all 13 of them)

> 7. We believe in the gift of tongues, **prophecy, revelation, visions**, healing, interpretation of tongues, and so forth.
>
> 12. **We believe in being subject to kings**, presidents, rulers, and magistrates, in obeying, honoring, and sustaining the law.

Also, if you read Article of Faith #12 above, it says Mormons believe in being subject to kings, and obeying their rules, in short, obey everything your told by ANYONE in authority. Fuck that! I can't even stand to be subject to corrupt "democratic" politicians who accept bribes (AKA campaign contributions), much less some asshole who was born into his/her position.

So, if the Mormon prophet, or one of his 12 Apostles says something, IT IS the word of god according to Mormons. That is how I took the advice from the church's pamphlet on Masturbation.

If you were to look at my class photos from when I was a young kid, you'll notice I was the smallest or at least one of the smallest kids in the class, which meant I would be a "late bloomer" when it came to hitting puberty. When you're forced to shower after physical education class in a large open shower, there's no where to hide. I'd notice that some kids started to grow hair in places I hadn't yet. I eventually did though, and started to notice my body making some changes.

I guess it was about this time that I started to pay more attention to my penis, and I noticed it seemed to feel nice when I would touch it in certain ways. However, one day when I was 13 years old and touching myself in the shower, I achieved orgasm/ejaculation for the very first time. This was an amazing experience, and one that I would surely want to do again.

Since the Mormon church already told its members that nude pictures, like those found in Playboy Magazine, were very bad, I was sure that what I was doing was not an "approved of" activity, and thus the internal conflict began. I was able to conceal my masturbating for a while, but when I was 15 years old and visiting some family out of state, I found a magazine in the bathroom trash with pictures of naked women. This was like hitting the jackpot for a young kid with no means to acquire that kind of material on my own (pre-Internet days). As I looked at the pictures of the beautiful naked women, I pleasured myself, but needed someplace to ejaculate, so I did it in the magazine, then put the magazine back in the trash.

Well, apparently the person who threw the magazine away, got it out of the trash later, and noticed pages sticking together (from my semen). Knowing I was the only other male in the house, it was not too difficult to figure out what I had done. I was confronted with this and admitted my guilt. They also told my parents (or at least my mom), and basically pressured me into confessing this sin to my local Mormon bishop when I returned home to Wasilla Alaska a few weeks later.

The bishop basically said I needed to repent, stop masturbating, stop looking at pictures of naked women, stop having sexual thoughts about women, and not partake of the sacrament on Sunday of any week in which I committed these sins. The part about not taking the sacrament on Sunday during church was a big deal. After all, I was 15, held the lower version of the priesthood called the "Aaronic Priesthood", and was not only supposed to take the sacrament (a little piece of bread and water), I was supposed to be helping to distribute the sacrament to the congregation and/or prepare it before church. While I didn't have to say WHY I could not partake of the sacrament, or help pass it out, I did have to inform my priesthood leaders and other boys my age that I could not help them pass it out. This is a very public shaming for something as natural as eating, urinating or defecating, in addition to the shame I felt every time I masturbated in private.

From the ages of 15 to 19, I moved a few times and each time I had to re-confess my sin of masturbating to my new bishop. I actually had one bishop say that masturbating in and of itself was not that bad of a sin, but the major sin was the sexual thoughts I would have while masturbating and/or the viewing of pictures of women in various stages of undress. So, what this bishop was telling me was that it was OK to masturbate, as long as I don't have sexual fantasies. What am I supposed to think about while masturbating? Toasters, math, sports? This is really fucked up advise, and not emotionally healthy in any way.

The summer I turned 16, my family moved from Wasilla Alaska, to Provo Utah. Many non-Mormons probably think that Salt Lake City, which is the capital of Utah, to be the heart of Mormonville, but that is not true at all. The center of the holier-than-thou Mormons is Provo Utah, where Brigham Young University (BYU) is located. I soon learned that many in Provo viewed Salt Lake City and some of its suburbs as "sin city".

What really ticked me off about Provo, was that the people there thought they lived in paradise. I had just lived in Alaska for the previous 5 years and had been on numerous boy scout outings and had seen some really spectacular scenery up there. Provo, with its polluted lake you could not swim it, and treeless mountain range was pretty ugly to me.

While I was born and raised Mormon, I was not prepared for the amount of conformity I found in Provo. I felt like I was suffocating, and this is back in the day when I totally believed in the church. A prime example of this "Taliban like" conformity was one warm sunny day my mother asked me to drive my sisters up to BYU where she was attending college so we could all grab something to eat. Since it was a hot sunny day, I was wearing shorts, a t-shirt and tennis shoes. When we arrived, my mom said I had to go back home and change since my shorts were too short for the BYU dress code.

I was confused. I wore these shorts all the time, even when playing church basketball. The issue at BYU was that you CAN wear shorts, but they must cover all of your leg down to your knee. Basically, you can wear shorts which just expose your calves and kneecaps. Anything else is immodest. The actual reason for this is not modesty, but their "magic underwear". Adult Mormons who attend the temple, have to wear special undergarments. They are sometimes referred to as "magic underwear" because the Mormon leaders tell their members that these undergarments will protect them from physical harm, as long as they wore them at all times and obeyed all of the church rules.

Anyway, BYU assumes that many of its students have been to the temple, and thus make everyone wear long shorts so the ones who are wearing magic Mormon underwear can cover their magic undergarments and not look out of place, since everyone has to wear the long shorts.

For me, I still thought this was bullshit. Sure I was Mormon, but only 16 and would not be able to go to the temple until I was 19, so why the fuck were they making me cover ½ of my legs, when there was no reason to?

Growing up, going through puberty, dealing with acne and other things was difficult enough, but when the church shames you for masturbating, which is as normal as peeing when your bladder is full, and making you feel like you'll go to their version of hell if you have natural reproductive thoughts about the opposite sex while physically interacting with your own body, is not only bullshit, but psychological abuse.

I figured out the Mormon church was bullshit when I was 20 years old and serving as a church missionary in San Diego, California. Do you have any idea what it's like to suddenly realize that for the last 7 years I had been under a tremendous guilt trip for nothing! I was so pissed off about this, that even now, 28 years later I still get bitter inside just thinking of that crap and how my younger years may have been a little more well adjusted if it wasn't for that damn church.

In 2002, I made a trip to Provo Utah, climbed up to the big "Y" on the side of the mountain and told Provo, BYU and the Mormon church they were all #1 (in my own special way).

Other Bullshit:

[29] Anti-Depressant Medications

Have you ever had the feeling like your world was falling apart? Well, this started happening to me in the late 1990's. I had already been in college for about 5 years, attending full-time, part-time, had switched majors, had to retake a few classes I had not passed the first time, etc... When I first started school, I was offered multiple credit cards with large credit limits, and student loans, and was using them to live off of, in addition to working in the summers and sometimes in the school year. School was a real struggle I was not sure I would succeed at, but was determined to give it everything I had.

For spring break of 1998, my girlfriend and I went on a road trip. This trip, started in Boise Idaho during the daylight hours when it was warm, so I was wearing shorts and a t-shirt. Shortly after dark, traveling on a two lane highway in the middle of nowhere, I thought I spotted something off of the road. As we got closer, my attention was drawn to a large vehicle which was off the road. I turned my attention back to the road, then had to swerve a few times to avoid running over chunks of tire. I could immediately tell that something was wrong, so I turned the car around and parked behind a semi-truck that was parked along the side of the road.

I told my girlfriend to stay put, and I went to talk to the driver of the parked semi-truck, to see what was going on, and if any assistance was needed. He unrolled his window a little, but I could tell he was talking to someone on the CB Radio, or cell phone, so I waited a moment until he got out of his vehicle. Apparently, he had been following another semi-truck and they were both headed in the opposite direction from me, and the truck in front of him suffered a left front tire blowout, which caused it to swerve left, crossing the oncoming traffic lane, went completely off the road, and subsequently rolled over so it was now upside down.

It was completely dark out, so I got a flashlight from my girlfriend's car, and went to investigate the wreck along with the driver from the other truck. This semi-truck had gone off of the road only minutes before, and we were the very first people to respond to it. I had no idea what to expect, but started to make my way through the sagebrush shining my flashlight around looking for any people who might need assistance.

I went on one side of the overturned semi-truck and the other driver searched the opposite side of the vehicle. Pretty quickly I spotted some clothing, and went closer to investigate. My immediate reaction was that I had found a body, not a living person, and I yelled to the other driver to come over.

Apparently, when the front left tire blew out, the semi-truck veered to the left across the oncoming traffic (but no cars were hit, or even around), turned over, the contents of the flat bed it was towing scattered, and the cab of the truck was then crushed, but while being crushed, the driver was partially outside of his side window and thus got pinned in a way that when the truck came to a stop, his head, right arm and part of his chest were sticking out from under the truck, was face up and his hand/wrist were covering his eyes. He had the painful expression of someone who had just had a semi-truck land on his chest, but his eyes were covered.

I had seen a few dead bodies before... I had seen a few relatives who had passed away from old age in their funeral caskets. My older sister's friend, a senior in high school, who lived a few houses down from us in Anchorage had committed suicide in her car and I saw her body slumped out of the drivers side door. I also saw the legs of some man who had been shot across the street from our house in Wasilla. However, I saw the bodies of the murder and suicide from a certain distance (from the street), didn't see any facial expressions, and I was also not the first person to find them dead like was the case with this truck accident.

You never really know how you will handle a situation like this. Sure my first instinct was that this guy was definitely dead, and the other driver didn't second guess this, but I had not attempted to take a pulse or make any other physical contact to see if he was just knocked unconscious.

I was able to walk around the body, get down on my hands and knees right next to him, and didn't see any signs of breathing or any movement, only one small drop of blood slowly moving down one of his fingers, but the blood didn't seem to originate from any wound I could see. However, to take this guy's pulse, I would need to move his arm which was covering his eyes. He had a painful expression on his face, and to move his arm would expose his eyes and thus his full facial expression and this scared me really bad. So much so, that I was unable to ever touch him at all.

I was able to look for other people/bodies, since we were not sure if this one body was the only one or not. Peeking through the twisted metal, I was able to see a foot and part of a leg, but was able to determine that given the distance and orientation to the body, it belonged to the dead driver and not someone else.

After searching all around the overturned semi-truck, the other driver and I were able to determine that there didn't seem to be any other bodies, at least ones we could see from all the wreckage, and the other driver indicated that he told the highway patrol that he would stay there until they arrived, but I was free to go if I wanted. I was not about to leave this guy alone, so I stayed awhile longer.

My body started to shake, and I was aware that this could be because of shock and/or the cold, as it was chilly out, and I was just wearing shorts, a t-shirt and tennis shoes. Then, from the road I heard my girlfriend start her car, and I was thinking where the hell is she going? Apparently, some other people had pulled over to see what was going on, and told her to go call for help, not being aware that the other truck driver had already done that.

So, I started to make my way back up to the road, and noticed a few people walking towards the wreckage with flashlights. I got into my girlfriends car, let her know that she didn't need to go get help, and warmed up a little with the car heater. The shaking stopped, and since the other truck driver had said I could go, and other people were now with him, and I had not actually witnessed the accident happen, and didn't touch anything, I figured it was OK to continue on our trip, so that is what we did.

We drove for about another hour before reaching our destination that evening. We had not eaten dinner yet, so we went to go get some food. Walking around the restaurant and the building attached to it, I could not get it out of my mind. What are all these people doing just walking around like nothing had changed. I'm aware that they had no idea of the accident, but it was just weird that the world just kept going on as normal.

The next morning while taking a shower a thought popped into my head. What if the driver of that semi-truck was not really dead and was just unconscious from hitting his head or something like that. If this was the case, I had failed him in the worse way, since I found him, was unable to touch him to check his pulse, and left. While I had been fairly certain he was dead at the scene, I was starting to have doubts.

The trip that my girlfriend and I were on was just beginning, and in a few days we would be traveling back the same way we came, and would have to go right past the scene of the accident again. My thoughts kept focusing on the accident. I'd think maybe he was alive right now in a hospital. I thought about the fact that about 9 miles before we arrived at the accident scene, we had stopped quickly for a restroom break and while starting on the road again, I had noticed 2 police cars off the side of the road near a street lamp and they were talking to each other (driver's doors facing each other). Because of this, I had driven about 5 miles per hour slower than I would have otherwise. If I had been traveling 5 miles per hour faster for approximately 9 miles, would I have seen the accident happen, would I have passed through the area before the wreck happened, or what if I would have been hit head-on by the semi-truck as it crossed over my lane.

The speed limit on that road was 70 miles per hour, and was fairly straight and flat. I'm sure the driver was probably going at least that fast, and when you take such a large heavy object and grind it along the ground a lot of dirt and vegetation will get turned up. This smell of fresh dirt and sage brush was very strong, and takes me back to the scene whenever I smell it.

A few days after the accident, on our way back home, we drove past the exact place it had occurred, but this time it was daylight. The whole area looked like it had been excavated and fresh dirt was plowed level everywhere. We didn't stop though.

After getting back to Boise, all of these things were going through my head, and I was not certain if the guy had actually died or not. So, I called someone from the highway patrol / dispatch who was aware of what had happened. I explained that I had been there, but was having second thoughts about if they guy had died or not. The lady confirmed that yes, it was a very bad accident, and yes the guy died at the scene.

Now, at least I knew that I had not left some guy who might have needed my help, but I had the overwhelming feeling like I had failed this guy. I should have been able to touch the guy, move his arm and take his pulse, either on his wrist or neck.

Then I'd think that here was this guy, driving his truck down the highway, then all of a sudden he gets a flat tire and seconds later is dead, just like that. Seems so trivial dying because of a flat tire. I could think of many situations in my life where I could have died if things didn't go just right, like the time when I was a baby and my older brother and/or sister fed me a quarter shaped metal plug from an electrical box and my mother came into the room and noticed I could not breath, was turning colors and she cleared it from my airway. When I was 4, I lived in a very unstable Northern Ireland (1975), then from ages 5-11, I lived just down stream from the Hanford Nuclear Plant in Richland Washington, the most nuclear contaminated location in America. Or, what about the time when I was 16 and driving my mom's car and lost control of it. The car spun around 360 degrees, then another 180, yet failed to hit anything, stayed upright and also stayed on the roadway. Then there was the time in the winter of 1992/93 in Beluga River Alaska, when the small twin engine plane I was riding in landed on a runway of black ice, and took 99.999% of the runway to come to a stop and had slid sideways the last bit of it. Or, what about the time I was camping with the boy scouts at the annual "Freezeree" in Alaska, and the temperature was well below zero and I could not stop shaking in my sleeping bag and was sure I'd freeze to death, but sure enough I woke up alive the next morning. I'd been through many situations which were more dangerous than a flat tire. I'd seen a fucking volcano (Mt. Spurr 1992) blow its top in person, and had ash from 2 others (Mt. Saint Helens in 1980 and St.

Augustine in 1986) fall on my head. I've been on an oil platform when an earthquake struck (summer of 1993, Baker oil platform in the Cook Inlet of Alaska). I'd not only been in a car that had a flat tire before, but drove a dune buggy which had its rear tire fall off, not once, but twice. Then, there was that time in 1993 when I was repelling in Boise Idaho as part a recreation/ROTC class I took my first semester, and while I was 1/3 of the way down, I noticed I could not move down anymore. I looked at my harness and noticed my carabiner was jammed open by the climbing rope. I was stuck there for a few minutes, a couple of stories above an asphalt parking lot (not the softest place to land). Lucky for me, the place we were repelling from had little windows, and they were able to reach my toe and pull me inside. I think you get the point. I've had many "close calls", where it would not have taken much at all to tweak the situation just a little and I'd be dead. Then there's this truck driver who died because of a fucking flat tire. It just didn't make any sense.

> Note: Technically, I don't have any recollection of the choking incident as a baby, but my mother wrote it down for me in my "Book of Remembrance" (a Mormon journal) from her point of view.

Anyway, the incident was over, and while pretty traumatic, I figured my life would return to normal in a few weeks. That didn't happen. Instead, I kept thinking about it... month after month, until the one year anniversary of it neared, then I started to think of it even more, and wondering why the fuck I couldn't get it out of my head.

The spring break a year after the accident, I was single and decided to go see an old friend in Utah and also my dad. As twilight was starting to settle in, I was driving through the same state as the truck accident a year earlier, but on a different road, and off in the distance I saw police lights flashing and I started to worry that maybe it's another accident. Fortunately it was just a police officer who had pulled someone over for speeding and not an accident. Later in the spring break, I went with my father to southern Utah, did some golfing, then went to see where one of our ancestors was killed. His name was John D. Lee and was one of the key figures in the Mountain Meadows Massacre and the only one to be punished for it (AKA shot to death). After leaving the memorial site for Mountain Meadows, I was driving down the road and thought I saw a motor cycle in the ditch. I drove a little further, then decided to turn back and investigate. There actually was a motorcycle in the ditch, but looked long abandoned and not some recent wreck.

With all these thoughts and reminders about death and the accident the year before, my mind was even more preoccupied than before. It was clear I was not getting better, but actually worse. I was not sure what to do, and up to that point had not sought help from a counselor. After spring break, I went to a counselor at Boise State, and told him what I was going through, and explained that when I attend my classes, I could not concentrate at all on what the teachers were saying. The BSU counselor said I was probably suffering from PTSD (Post Traumatic Stress Disorder), and he approved an academic withdrawal from that semester of school.

I packed up my few belongings and went to go live with my brother in Oregon. However, this was just the start of everything going bad. My poor financial decisions in the past were starting to catch up with me and becoming a problem. My credit cards were maxed out, I didn't have a job, and my brother was charging me to stay at his house, so I was not living any cheaper than if I had my own place.

I tried to look for work in Oregon, and even had an interview for some tech support job lined up, but I was such a mess, that on the day I was supposed to go to the job interview I got lost trying to find the place and eventually pulled over to the side of the road and just cried.

At my request, my mother traveled to see me, and she then accompanied me on a two day trip to go back to scene of the truck accident more than a year earlier. I was not sure exactly what I was doing, but hoping to make some peace with myself. I purchased some flowers for the trip and was planning on planting them where the man had died. When we arrived at the site of the accident, most of the excavated dirt now had light vegetation starting to grow through, but the actual location where the semi-truck had come to a stop was still easy to find and had zero vegetation. The last time I had seen the place, which was a few days after accident on our way back to Boise, there was lots of fresh excavated dirt, so I didn't think to bring a shovel, but now the dirt was fairly hard... too hard to dig a small hole using my hands to plant the flowers in.

After wondering around a little, I started to notice bits and pieces of the truck which had been left behind by the cleanup crew. Not big pieces, but little stuff scattered about. I found the hook part of a tie-down strap, which had clearly been ripped during the accident, and was able to use this piece of metal to dig a hole large enough to plant the flowers at the exact spot I had found this man's body. I sat for awhile, said some things and in general was asking for forgiveness for my weakness and inability to take his pulse.

I think that going there was good for me. I was able to return to the exact same spot, but instead of it being dark and cold outside, the sun was shinning and the body and truck wreckage were no longer there. This however would not even be close to the end of my issues.

Things were not really working out living with my brother, and I was also running out of money really fast. It was becoming apparent that my credit card debt was starting to snowball so fast that I could no longer even keep up with the interest payments. Since I had not graduated from college yet, I didn't have many options for getting a job that would pay well enough for me to handle this debt.

Being an emotional mess and broke, I was talked into moving back to Boise Idaho to live with my ex-girlfriend. The living arraignments would be a little awkward though, as she was now pregnant and living with the father of the soon to be baby. To say this was a weird living arraignment is putting it mildly, but I guess she realized that I had not been the same since the truck wreck and probably had some sympathy for me.

After returning to Boise and moving in with my pregnant ex-girlfriend and her new boyfriend, I filed for bankruptcy to clear 35K worth of credit card debt. I also had approximately 30K in student loan debt, but that does not come off with a bankruptcy. I then found a job working the night shift at Micron Technology, where I helped run an assembly line which built memory modules (like the ones you find in your computer).

After a few months of that living arraignment, I was ready to move out of my ex-girlfriends place and tried to rent an apartment, but they asked to give them references for previous landlords and also to do a credit check. They called me back a few days later with two items of bad news. First, the landlady I had previously rented from in Boise had apparently recently died in a car wreck, and second, because I had a bankruptcy on my record, they could not rent to me.

This was crazy. I had rented from this lady for awhile. She was also nice enough to let me out of my lease so I could go live with my brother in Oregon. Now, a few months later, I find out she was in a car wreck, which was caused because she was distracted from her cell phone, then when her car flipped, she was not wearing her seat-belt, which resulted in her death.

I eventually found a place that would rent to me and I was able to move out from my pregnant ex-girlfriends place, so her and her new boyfriend could make a decent attempt at their relationship.

This was not the only bad news around that time. I heard back from Boise State, and although they originally said I was fine to drop out of college due to my circumstances, they changed their mind, and instead of having my classes that semester marked with a "W" for withdrawal, they were all changed to "F" for fail. This pissed me off really fucking bad. I had asked BSU if I could withdrawal for PTSD issues, they said yes, go ahead and leave, then after I had actually moved, they changed their minds. This is betrayal at its very worst, because if they had said no to begin with, I may have made a different decision, but since they said yes it was OK to leave, I went down that path, only to have them pull the rug from under me once I made my move.

Anyway, I now had a job which gave me health benefits, and as part of this I was able to afford to go to a counselor for all the issues I was going through. I found 2 people; one was a psychiatrist who would give me medications, and the other was a psychologist who would do counseling sessions with me. Both worked in the same office and would share notes on my progress, or lack thereof.

So here I was, working full-time nights, seeing a counselor, and getting some meds for PTSD and depression from a psychiatrist. I had not yet flunked out of school, so BSU allowed me to return and I did so part time. However, working full-time nights and going to school part-time in the day, is really too much. This went on for a few semesters, but eventually my grades dropped below a certain point and BSU sent me an official letter saying I had "flunked out of school" after the fall semester of 2000 and they would not allow me to return for at least one year. If that one semester in question had "W" instead of "F" for all those classes, my GPA would still be good enough, so that was more salt in the wounds.

The drugs my psychiatrist was giving me were NOT working. I was still very depressed and getting worse as time went on.

While I had always been fairly fit all my life, I packed on 40 lbs in a short amount of time and some of the medications made it next to impossible to reach orgasm/ejaculation. So not only does my life suck, these meds had now made me fat and the one thing that I used to get some satisfaction from (Masturbating and/or Sex) was not even working properly anymore.

My psychiatrist would change my meds every so often after realizing that the current meds or doses for the meds were not working for me. Going on and off anti-depressants and other meds for PTSD, is not as simple as stopping one and starting another. You have to wean yourself off of one by lowering the dosage over the course of about a week, then ramp up slowly on the new one, and I did this multiple times while trying to find medication(s) that would work for me.

One time, the new meds made me VERY irritable. I would find myself driving down the road and someone in another lane ahead of me would put on their blinker to indicate they wanted to pull in front of me, but if they were anywhere near me at all, I'd freak out and flash my lights at them and flip them off and really was on the edge of road rage. I would have also used my car's horn, but it didn't work. It didn't take very long with that specific medication to realize it was bad for me. I contacted my psychiatrist and demanded to be taken off of that one completely. She wanted to try a lower dosage, but I feared I would have some sort of violent incident and was not willing to take that chance.

Another time, I got fed up with all of it and stopped taking my meds without the slow weaning off period and this was very bad as well. I could move my hand in front of my face, and instead of seeing a smooth motion, my hand would appear to skip as if frames in a movie had been taken out.

Over the course of a year or so I had been attending regular sessions with my psychologist, but was not making any progress and I was more or less a lost cause for her. I enjoyed chatting with her, but was so depressed that I was not willing to try any new social activities she thought would help me.

In early 2002, with things getting worse, my counselor hinted that it's possible I could be admitted to the local mental hospital, where they could be more aggressive in finding better medications for my PTSD and depression. I thought about it for awhile, then decided what the fuck, I'll give it a try.

Turns out, she either didn't know what she was talking about, or was just worried I might attempt suicide and was just trying to get me to a safe place where that would not occur. I checked myself into the hospital voluntarily, but soon realized this was not only really fucking expensive, but they were not really planning on making med changes, just keeping me under observation.

Before I went into the mental hospital, I had no idea how long I would be there, so I had contacted one of my sisters to let her know. She then contacted my parents and siblings, and many of them showed up in Boise to visit me in the hospital. This is not what I had planned and was hoping to keep it to myself and maybe a select few people.

When life sucks really bad, the last thing that will make you feel better is a huge medical bill. When I checked in, they didn't really discuss the fee, just saying something like "what's it worth to you, to get healthy again", or some shit like that. I was lucky and I believe family members picked up that bill for me.

When I got out of the hospital 5 days later, my parents and siblings convinced me to leave Boise and my night job and go stay with one of them.

Since I no longer had a job, my medical insurance ran out a few months later (sometime in spring/summer of 2002), and I could no longer afford the meds my psychiatrist had prescribed for me. At the time, I thought this was just one more piece of bad luck in my life, but turns out it was a blessing in disguise.

Not taking the meds did NOT make me happy again. However, all the side affects like excessive weight gain stopped, I was no longer having issues with achieving ejaculation/orgasm during masturbation, and no severe mood swings.

After bouncing around between various family members, I ended up staying with one of my siblings and working as a part-time janitor for her business. This living/work arraignment lasted for about 2.5 years.

During my time as a part-time janitor, the extra 40 lbs I had gained very quickly while I was taking the psychiatric meds, just stayed there. It didn't move up anymore, but it also didn't go away.

If I were to take an inventory of where my life was at that point I'd list these things:

- Suffering from PTSD.
- Suffering from Depression.
- Flunked out of college.
- Working as a part-time janitor.
- 40 lbs overweight.
- Had more than 30k of student loan debt that I could not pay off and it was just accumulating interest.
- Was driving a car with almost 200,000 miles on it.
- Hadn't been with a woman in a few years.
- Had bankruptcy on my credit report.
- Was living with family, since I could not afford my own place.

In other words, my life sucked really bad! The first few years after I had flunked out of college, I was bitter at the school for the way they betrayed me, and also had lost a lot of confidence in myself and wondered if I was smart enough, and basically had no plans to ever return. However, I guess that time lessens the pain a little and I started to think the only way to a better life was to finish my degree and get a decent paying job.

First however, I needed to clear up that one semester of "F's", which should have been "W's" (withdrawals instead of failing grades). This was a complete cluster fuck and is a story of its own. To make this real short, it took a LOT of work to convince BSU that they had fucked me over by telling me it was OK to leave school, then changing their minds later after I had already moved away. I had to take this issue all the way up to the BSU President, who had the authority to fix the mess.

During this phase of trying to come up with a plan to get my life back on track,

I cut out fast food, 99% of my soda-pop intake, 100% of alcohol, and also started running on my sister's treadmill. My thought was, "hey, you don't see fat people running marathons". It was a little rough at first, and I developed a sore knee, but eventually settled into an exercise plan that worked for me. I would run 2.2 miles, every other day, at a pace of 8 minutes per mile. I also walked a little before and after my runs.

Over the course of about 5-6 months I lost 40 lbs and was back to my normal healthy weight. However, much more important that losing the weight, I noticed that I had not been feeling down and depressed anymore. I had not been on any medications for depression, PTSD, or anything else for that matter in a few years, so it was not medications which made me feel better.

After almost 9 years of hindsight, I've been able to re-examine what exactly it was that helped me beat back my depression and PTSD, and it definitely was NOT medication, but rather I believe it was a combination of these things:

- Running at a quick pace (8 minutes per mile) for a few miles every other day, really gets my heart and lungs active.
- Reducing/eliminating shitty foods like soda and fast food.
- Time
- Hope

That's it. Eat right, **get serious cardio exercise**, find some goal to strive for which will make your life better in the long run, and lastly the realization that even really bad things will fade from your daily thoughts, given enough time.

Warning: What I've described here is what worked for me from 2004-2008. Later on, in December of 2015, I attempted suicide, but I had not been running regularly in a few years due to physical issues (tight/sore muscles and joints).

If you're currently on medications for depression and/or PTSD, and it's working for you, that is awesome. However, if your medications are not working, **talk to your doctor** about the things I've described above that worked for me.

Also, an 8 minute mile is a fairly intense workout and not everybody can handle this. Use caution and consult with your doctor before starting this.

Next I had to figure out how to pay for my return to school. I figured my two best options were:

1. Join the army, and see if they would either pay for my school, or train me as a computer programmer.
2. Go work for my dad in construction.

Although solution #1 did have some nice financial incentives at the time (2005), I was skeptical of it. I was not guaranteed to be a computer programmer, and also the recruiters knew of my 5 day stint in the mental hospital, and basically said they could overlook this, but if I ran into issues later on regarding depression and/or PTSD, they would claim they had no knowledge of my previous issues and would claim that I had covered it up on my application. This is however why I started running in the first place, to get into shape in case I would have to go to boot camp.

I ended up going with option #2 and worked for my dad as a stone mason for 5 months before my first semester back at BSU, and also the 2 summers after that.

It had been 4.5 years since I had flunked out of college, and just returning to school was not going to be good enough. If I repeated what I had done before, I was setting myself up for possible failure again. I was extremely determined to make it work this time around, so I wrote down a "Plan for Success in School".

This plan include things like:

- No working and attending school at same time.
- No drinking.
- No dating.
- Limit the number of classes I take so I can avoid getting overwhelmed.
- Run every other day.

I would read this "Plan for Success in School" once a week to remind myself of what I needed to do, else risk failure again. For the most part I stuck to this plan and it worked. Over a span of 2.5 years, I attended BSU part-time, worked 60 hour weeks in the summers as a stone mason, and maintained a 3.4

GPA in my remaining classes (only A's and B's) and finally, 14 ½ years after I had attended my first college course, I graduated on December 21st, 2007 with a B.S. in Computer Science.

Six months after graduating, I had 2 separate job offers to go work AT Microsoft, but not FOR Microsoft, but if you've read the previous chapters, you already know that story. A few months after I started this contract job at Microsoft, the economy collapsed (fall of 2008). I had spent all this time working my ass off to get my life together, a college education and a decent paying job, just to find out that whoever was running this world had fucked it all up. How do you think I felt about that?

Instead of looking at the superficial reasons for the economic collapse like sub-prime housing loans and Wall Street, I tried to find the root cause of the failure. What was it, that lead to all of this bullshit? After awhile, I was able to determine that America's main issue is that its politicians don't actually represent its population, but rather the rich and powerful who bribe them with campaign contributions. Sure there are other places in the world that suck much more than we do, but that does not change the fact that *The United States of America* is NOT a democracy (or even a "constitutional republic"), it's a corruptocracy!

[30] Conclusion

What is knowledge? Knowledge is simply information you know, which may or may not be true. A dictionary, which is just a list of words and their meanings, is an example of knowledge you might know or have access to. Having access to knowledge is important, but being able to analyze and understand the knowledge is MUCH more important.

When I was a young kid, I was told Santa Clause would know if I was naughty or nice, was able to visit every house on the planet in one evening and fit through the chimney to deliver presents.

Was this knowledge about Santa Clause true or false? False of course, but how did I figure out that this information, given to me by people I trusted, was false? When I was in Kindergarten, someone who was dressed up as Santa Clause came to visit our class and asked each of us what we wanted for Christmas. I told Santa that I wanted a truck. He asked if I wanted one I could drive, and I thought he was crazy, since in my mind, I thought he was referring to one like my dad drove around, and not the small little electric toy vehicles made just big enough for kids to sit in.

Anyway, while walking home from school that day with my cousin, I mentioned to her that Santa Clause looked a lot like the school principle. I was then able to determine, that all he had to do was tell our parents what we asked him for Christmas, then our parents could buy that gift and place it under the tree and pretend that it came from Santa Clause.

This ability to take the knowledge I had been given as a child, by supposedly trusted people, analyze it with what I observed around me, then determine the knowledge I had was not accurate, is what we call intelligence.

This entire book, is simply me applying my intelligence (AKA problem solving skills) to other topics which many humans on this planet seem unable to figure out on their own.

In this book, I've pointed out many instances of bullshit in the world today, almost all of which is a direct result of NOT having political leaders which actually represent the people. I called this "corruptocracy". I've given you very simple yet specific solutions to the following problems:

1. Described how to create a real democracy where money has ZERO influence over the election process, and in doing so, removed 99% of political corruption which is currently built into the U.S. Government.

2. I pointed out very horrible employment practices by large corporations

like Microsoft and Apple, then designed the *Turing Employment Center*, which eliminates ALL discrimination in the employment hiring process, something that laws and good intentions alone will NEVER be able to do.

3. I provided a simple step-by-step solution to prove that NOBODY, not even the Mormon Prophet, can actually heal people simply by placing their hands on the head of a sick person and saying a prayer (or god heal the sick person through them).

4. I challenged the way we currently educate the new humans coming into this world, and provided an outline of how to create a better learning system.

5. I pointed out how the Mormon church (and possibly other people/organizations) shames its young people for a bodily act that is as normal as eating, urinating and defecating. I then provided some ideas on how to instruct them that this is normal, nothing to be ashamed of, and also provided the 3 *Stages of Permission* to reduce unwanted physical contact among humans.

6. Resolved the question of who was right/wrong between religion and atheism.

– Isaac Benson Powell

Appendix A: The "13 Articles of Faith" of the Mormon Church

1. We believe in God, the Eternal Father, and in His Son, Jesus Christ, and in the Holy Ghost.

2. We believe that men will be punished for their own sins, and not for Adam's transgression.

3. We believe that through the Atonement of Christ, all mankind may be saved, by obedience to the laws and ordinances of the Gospel.

4. We believe that the first principles and ordinances of the Gospel are: first, Faith in the Lord Jesus Christ; second, Repentance; third, Baptism by immersion for the remission of sins; fourth, Laying on of hands for the gift of the Holy Ghost.

5. We believe that a man must be called of God, by prophecy, and by the laying on of hands by those who are in authority, to preach the Gospel and administer in the ordinances thereof.

6. We believe in the same organization that existed in the Primitive Church, namely, apostles, prophets, pastors, teachers, evangelists, and so forth.

7. We believe in the gift of tongues, prophecy, revelation, visions, healing, interpretation of tongues, and so forth.

8. We believe the Bible to be the word of God as far as it is translated correctly; we also believe the Book of Mormon to be the word of God.

9. We believe all that God has revealed, all that He does now reveal, and we believe that He will yet reveal many great and important things pertaining to the Kingdom of God.

10. We believe in the literal gathering of Israel and in the restoration of the Ten Tribes; that Zion (the New Jerusalem) will be built upon the American continent; that Christ will reign personally upon the earth; and, that the earth will be renewed and receive its paradisiacal glory.

11. We claim the privilege of worshiping Almighty God according to the dictates of our own conscience, and allow all men the same privilege, let them worship how, where, or what they may.

12. We believe in being subject to kings, presidents, rulers, and magistrates, in obeying, honoring, and sustaining the law.

13. We believe in being honest, true, chaste, benevolent, virtuous, and in doing good to all men; indeed, we may say that we follow the admonition of Paul-We believe all things, we hope all things, we have endured many things, and hope to be able to endure all things. If there is anything virtuous, lovely, or of good report or praiseworthy, we seek after these things.

Appendix B: Apple CEO's Racist and Sexist Statement

U.S. Race and Ethnicity Overall

White 55% Asian 15% Hispanic 11% Black 7% Two or More 2% Other 1% Undeclared 9%

U.S. Race and Ethnicity in Non-Tech

White 56%
Hispanic 14%
Asian 9%
Black 9%
Two or More 3%
Undeclared 9%

U.S. Race and Ethnicity in Tech

White 54%
Asian 23%
Hispanic 7%
Black 6%
Two or More 2%
Undeclared 8%

U.S. Race and Ethnicity in Leadership

White 64%
Asian 21%
Hispanic 6%
Black 3%
Undeclared 6%

Global Gender Overall

Male 70%
Female 30%

A Message from Tim Cook.

At Apple, our 98,000 employees share a passion for products that change people's lives, and from the very earliest days we have known that diversity is critical to our success. We believe deeply that inclusion inspires innovation.

Our definition of diversity goes far beyond the traditional categories of race, gender, and ethnicity. It includes personal qualities that usually go unmeasured, like sexual orientation, veteran status, and disabilities. Who we are, where we come from, and what we've experienced influence the way we perceive issues and solve problems. We believe in celebrating that diversity and investing in it.

Apple is committed to transparency, which is why we are publishing statistics about the race and gender makeup of our company. Let me say up front: As CEO, I'm not satisfied with the numbers on this page. They're not new to us, and we've been working hard for quite some time to improve them. We are making progress, and we're committed to being as innovative in advancing diversity as we are in developing our products.

Inclusion and diversity have been a focus for me throughout my time at Apple, and they're among my top priorities as CEO. I'm proud to work alongside the many senior executives we've hired and promoted in the past few years, including Eddy Cue and Angela Ahrendts, Lisa Jackson and Denise Young-Smith. The talented leaders on my staff come from around the world, and they each bring a unique point of view based on their experience and heritage. And our board of directors is stronger than ever with the addition of Sue Wagner, who was elected in July.

I receive emails from customers around the world, and a name that comes up often is Kim Paulk. She's a Specialist at the Apple Store on West 14th Street in Manhattan. Kim has a medical condition that has impaired her vision and hearing since she was a child. Our customers rave about Kim's service, and they say she embodies the best characteristics of Apple. Her guide dog, Gemma, is affectionately known around the store as the "seeing iDog."

When we think of diversity, we think of individuals like Kim. She inspires her coworkers and her customers as well.

We also think of Walter Freeman, who leads a procurement team here in Cupertino and was recently recognized by the National Minority Supplier Development Council. Last year, Walter's team provided over $3 billion in business opportunities with Apple to more than 7,000 small businesses in the western United States.

Both Walter and Kim exemplify what we value in diversity. Not only do they enrich the experience of their coworkers and make our business stronger, but they extend the benefits of Apple's diversity to our customers, into our supply chain and the broader economy. And there are many more people at Apple doing the same.

Above all, when we think of the diversity of our team, we think of the values and ideas they bring with them as individuals. Ideas drive the innovation that makes Apple unique, and they deliver the level of excellence our customers have come to expect.

Beyond the work we do creating innovative tools for our customers, improving education is one of the best ways in which Apple can have a meaningful impact on society. We recently pledged $100 million to President Obama's ConnectED initiative to bring cutting-edge technologies to economically disadvantaged schools. Eighty percent of the student population in the schools we will equip and support are from groups currently underrepresented in our industry.

Apple is also a sponsor of the Human Rights Campaign, the country's largest LGBT rights organization, as well as the National Center for Women & Information Technology, which is encouraging young women to get involved in technology and the sciences. The work we do with these groups is meaningful and inspiring. We know we can do more, and we will.

This summer marks the anniversary of the U.S. Civil Rights Act of 1964 — an opportunity to reflect on the progress of the past half-century and acknowledge the work that remains to be done. When he introduced the bill in June 1963, President Kennedy urged Congress to pass it "for the one plain, proud and priceless quality that unites us all as Americans: a sense of justice."

All around the world, our team at Apple is united in the belief that being different makes us better. We know that each generation has a responsibility to build upon the gains of the past, expanding the rights and freedoms we enjoy to the many who are still striving for justice.

Together, we are committed to diversity within our company and the advancement of equality and human rights everywhere.

Tim

Race and ethnicity data as of June 28, 2014; gender data as of August 2, 2014. Data supplied by Apple Human Resources.

"Every truth passes through three stages before it is recognized.
In the first, it is ridiculed.
In the second, it is opposed.
In the third, it is regarded as self evident."

- Arthur Schopenhauer

About the Author

Isaac Benson Powell holds a Bachelor of Science degree in Computer Science, from Boise State University (2007).

He is the developer of "Contachit", a computer language and IDE, which allows the user to read/write computer code in a flow-chart.

Born in Denver Colorado, the family he grew up in moved often due to his fathers work. By the time he started kindergarten, he had already lived in 3 countries (United States of America, England, and Northern Ireland). Since then, he has moved up and down the west coast of the United States, but out of all those places, the only place he calls "home" is Alaska.

It wasn't until he was 40 years old did he figure out what his passion in life was; Robotics. All it took was reading one book on the subject and assembling the small, line following robot described in it to know that was what he wanted to do for the rest of his life, knowing full well that he has much to learn, but that would be part of the journey.

Websites:

Personal	https://isaac-benson-powell.com
Contachit	https://contachit.com
This Book	https://corruptocracy.com

Hatcher Pass, Alaska 2014

www.ingramcontent.com/pod-product-compliance
Lightning Source LLC
Chambersburg PA
CBHW030602020526
44112CB00048B/1183